TEARS OF LOVE

PATTI CULLEN

LITTLE CREEK PRESS
AND BOOK DESIGN

MINERAL POINT, WISCONSIN

Little Creek Press.
5341 Sunny Ridge Road
Mineral Point, WI 53565

ORDERING INFORMATION
Quantity sales. Special discounts are available on quantity purchases by corporations, associations, and others. For details, contact info@littlecreekpress.com

Orders by US trade bookstores and wholesalers.
Please contact Little Creek Press or Ingram for details.

Printed in the United States of America

Cataloging-in-Publication Data
Names: Cullen, Patti, author
Title: Tears of Love
Description: Mineral Point, WI, Little Creek Press, 2023
Identifiers: LCCN: 2023921254 | ISBN: 978-1-955656-66-5
Subjects: REL077000 RELIGION / Faith
PSY037000 PSYCHOLOGY / Suicide
FAM014000 FAMILY & RELATIONSHIPS / Death, Grief, Bereavement

Book design by Little Creek Press

AUTHOR'S NOTE: *Tears of Love* is a nonfiction memoir created from journal entries after losing my son Benjamin, by suicide. While all the stories in this book are true, some names and identifying details have been changed to protect the privacy of the people involved. Everything written is based on my perception and may not be considered factual to those involved.

This book was written with the aspiration of reducing the stigma of suicide, aiding in suicide awareness and prevention, to share resources, and offer hope.

This book is for educational purposes only. It is not a substitute for seeking advice from a medical professional or healthcare provider for diagnosis or treatment.

The true heroes of any story are the survivors left behind to make sense of the unfathomable. If you're in pain or experiencing difficult thoughts, please call 988 to reach the Suicide and Crisis Lifeline. You're not alone.

This book is my story. I pray my story offers insight without judgement.

To Ben and all those that have died by suicide.
To all survivors who've lost a loved one to suicide.
To anyone struggling or contemplating suicide.

To my sister-in-law Connie Busch who died from cancer.
Connie was instrumental in our kids lives when they were
younger and supported our BENS Hope ministry
until her passing November 3, 2022.

FOREWORD

One of the main responsibilities associated with being a mother is being in a constant state of preparation. During our pregnancy, as we anxiously await the birth of our child, and as our belly grows, that sense of being prepared becomes more urgent until we reach the nesting phase. We make room in our home for our new addition, purchase diapers, buy a crib, and get art for the walls, a rocking chair for the nursery, and perhaps a stroller. Before we bring the baby home from the hospital, we make preparations for their homecoming by purchasing an age- and size-appropriate car seat. After bringing our beautiful child into the world, we experience the wondrous feeling of love at first sight as we cradle our beautiful baby in our arms for the very first time. The payoff for all these preparations becomes so vividly apparent. This child becomes an unending reason for love and the greatest blessing in our lives.

The duties of preparation continue as our child grows—we supply clothing, shoes, books, food, food, and more food. Then there are the school supplies, more clothes, the birthday parties, Christmas gifts, and of course, capturing these moments with photos, photos, and more photos, as well as videos, videos, and more videos! As moms, we always try to be prepared for what comes next as we care, comfort, and nurture our child through the good days, bad days, and all those in-between days. As our child grows from day one to the day they leave our nest, we offer them support as their biggest cheerleader, their "somebody who cares." Being a mom means we've trained ourselves to sacrifice our time and energy and to always be ready for their next call, text, email, Snapchat, Instagram message, or the most treasured interaction, an in-person visit from our child. And as moms, we hope all these years of preparation and building our best parenting skills can help us offer guidance to our child when they experience difficulties, whether related to friendships, a breakup, not getting the part, not making the team, or getting bullied.

It is when our child makes a plan of their own, one which they choose not to share, that throws a mom off course. On November 11, 2014, my beloved son and firstborn child, Benjamin, made such a plan, and since that day, my role as his mom would never be the same.

Throughout my life, certain situations have driven me to the brink where I sought out my faith. Once my faith served the purpose at hand, I carried on as usual, in control of my life, or so I thought. Becoming a mom for the first time found me seeking my faith again, due to unanticipated circumstances that complicated life. Over my course of years on this earth as a mom, I've learned that we all need to draw strength and patience from a source we can constantly rely on, especially in those instances when our energy tank is running low, we're emotionally, physically, and mentally drained, and our patience runs out. For my journey, God is my constant companion, which is why you'll see my faith surface frequently in this book. While my faith has been a part of my life for a while, it has been challenged at times, but it's also grown because of my circumstances.

My life coach, Tammy, asked me, "Whom are you writing this book for, who is your audience, or who do you hope will read this book?" After pondering, I concluded that my intention for writing this book is to reach the young and old, men and women, Christians or atheists, adults and children, people feeling happy, sad, or in between. Honestly, it's for any and everyone.

I believe life presents opportunities to help us grow and learn through our own circumstances and through the stories and experiences of others. Our story includes the death of our son, Benjamin, by suicide.

I know, it's the "S" word, one we'd rather stay away from. But what if instead of hiding from this topic or trying to protect your kids and staying away from this topic, you were given the opportunity to hear a story firsthand, our story, and learn from it? Parents like to hold others accountable for actions and behaviors their children experience, but what about us as parents? Are we doing the best we can to educate and protect them? Is the subject of suicide avoided because we don't think it will happen or because we're afraid it will? I'm not sure of your stance on the topic and have no intentions of judgment, but what I can share is that it is our responsibility to keep our children safe so that when something happens, we avoid pointing fingers at others, the schools, law enforcement, etc. We get it, suicide is *scary*, it involves *death*, but like Terry always says during our presentations, "Talk about suicide; it could save a life. I wish I would have talked with my son about suicide." And I guess we never did because we didn't think "it" would ever happen. But as we walk this walk daily, we have learned from those on a similar journey that they never thought it would happen either. That's why this book is being written—to help you understand it can happen and may happen, and avoiding the topic doesn't mean it won't happen. We pray however this book is meant to serve you, it does just that, whether you're the one struggling or you're helping a loved one who is struggling.

Tears of Love offers insight on lessons learned on my journey and why this book came to be. I share how my family came to deal with Benjamin's unexpected plan, how I am still in recovery—and always will be—and how his unanticipated action birthed a new and unexpected mission for my life.

CHAPTER 1

EXTRAORDINAIRE

*Be kind to one another, tenderhearted, forgiving one
another, even as God in Christ forgave you.*
Ephesians 4:32 (NKJV)

Extraordinaire. That's the one word my dear friend and colleague, Sarah, says she'd use to describe me. I associate the word "extraordinaire" with someone like a superhero, which I know I am not. There are days, though, when I encounter such extraordinary instances that make me pause and ponder how affirming my life's journey has been and where God is leading me next.

Early riser. That's the term I would use to describe myself. I'm one of those people who wakes up before the rising sun. I love to hear the birds sing and watch the sunrise. My husband of 39 years, Terry, shares a kiss with me as he heads out the door each morning to his job at UW-Platteville as a grounds crew lead. My mornings vary but typically start with an activity inside or out, weather permitting, since we live in Wisconsin. This may include a walk, walk/run, bike ride, yoga, or meditation. Regardless of which activity I choose, it involves time in prayer. Some mornings, prayer turns into meditation, and from there free writing, which offers me insight. Very intentionally, I pray throughout the day, at times without ceasing. I've relied on God to get me through many seasons in life. While I am blessed with loving family and friends, God has been my constant, especially since November 11, 2014.

In preparation for my day ahead, I also read from devotionals, listen to podcasts (I *love* Pastor Rick Warren), and tune in to Family Life Radio on 88.1 FM. These efforts have been instrumental in my survival on those darker and more difficult mornings. Skipping my morning devotionals would be like skipping out on God. Time and time again, He's always been there for me, so in turn, I offer myself to Him.

Regardless of which direction my morning takes me, my usual routine includes forecasting the day ahead of me. Of course, my review includes a rundown of our kids, their whereabouts, and what they have going on or coming up. I can't speak for others, but for me, our three children are the best gifts I've ever received. I don't take for granted the blessings they each are. We've also received another blessing recently, our precious grandbaby, Desiree, also called Desi, baby, Desi bear, sweetheart, beautiful, and all those lovely names grandparents use in adoration. Desiree's name derives from the word "desired," and I can promise that she was a long-awaited blessing and very much desired by our daughter, Carrie, and our wonderful son-in-law, Matt, as well as our entire family!

My morning rituals may be postponed or even bypassed if there is a deadline at work. As an assistant vice president and internal auditor at Mound City Bank in Platteville, Wisconsin, deadlines are part of my job. That may mean arriving early to work to wrap up audit reports, ensure replies are returned from management, and finalize agendas in preparation for the quarterly audit meetings with the Board of Directors (BOD). It's a priority in my heart to ensure I do my best work for the BOD, our shareholders, and my colleagues at our community-owned bank.

Terry and I were both raised as country kids in Platteville, Wisconsin, and came from Catholic families. I was one of five children and Terry one of thirteen. Terry and I are both in the middle of the pack of our siblings. After being high school sweethearts, we married in 1983 and were blessed with three children: Benjamin was born in 1987, Mandy in 1988, and Carrie in 1990. Needless to say, having a three-year-old, two-year-old, and newborn kept us busy! When we weren't busy running in circles with our kiddos, we enjoyed attending their extracurricular activities, with a great majority of our time —which, may I add, included weekends —spent on the sidelines of a soccer field. As our kids grew, our home became the gathering place where all of their friends socialized. I recall walking in the house, and seeing the entryway piled a mile high with an array of shoes. Life was full of chaos, and now we cherish those special memories.

Upon their graduations, Ben attended Southwest Technical College before moving to La Crosse, Wisconsin. Mandy ventured to La Crosse; Des Moines, Iowa; Boulder, Colorado, and back to Madison before landing in Blue Mounds, Wisconsin. Carrie went from Eau Claire, Wisconsin, to Minnesota and then ended up in Madison. Life was exciting as we witnessed our kids striving and thriving, just as parents hope and pray for. We were proud of their accomplishments and looked forward to the exciting milestones ahead. Little did we know the fate in front of us and what our reality would become.

My day typically begins by 5:00 a.m.. If I want to be at work by 5:00, my day starts earlier. Some days, I go to work as late as 8:00 a.m. My days consist of writing audit reports, attending meetings, and performing audit tests. As an internal auditor, it's my responsibility to ensure regulations are adhered to, controls are enforced, and compliance is met. I work closely with Sarah, our compliance officer, who is also one of my favorite people. I also meet with an array of colleagues depending on the function under audit review. While most of my work is accomplished from our main office, some audits require travel to our branch offices located in and outside of the county. I also work closely with external auditors and facilitate exams with the regulators. Sounds like fun, right? Let's just say it wasn't a job I signed up for but was chosen for due to my eye for detail. I definitely had to tweak this position to align with my personality. My intentions and loyalty to the bank ensure I do my best as well as help others learn and grow to be and do their best. I'm not the typical stereotype of an auditor some perceive—someone peering over their glasses wedged at the front of their nose. No, that's definitely not me!

I owe the longevity of my career at the bank to the relationships I've built with my colleagues and the family-oriented environment our company is known for. I care deeply about them and have been blessed with some incredible friendships during my tenure since starting in 1979.

Typically, during my workday I encounter my colleagues and friends Barb, Sarah, and Sandy—who, like me and like each of you—have their own stories. While my friendships with Barb and Sarah were already strong to begin with, the loss of their moms deepened our friendships. Sandy and I became friends after her surgery. You see, Sandy was diagnosed with stage 4 brain cancer with melanoma and was given a 34 percent survival rate. Just like that, her life changed in an instant. I started visiting Sandy's office each morning to share a daily devotion from *Jesus Calling* by Sarah Young. Every day, the devotion seemed remarkably relevant to how we were both feeling that specific day. On days Sandy had follow-up appointments, I would offer a more special prayer that God put on my heart. It was a beautiful bonding experience in friendship and faith. Sandy is currently doing so well that she is on the doctor's short list of being a miracle.

I refer to Barb and Sarah as my "Earth Angels," which they truly are. There are not enough hours or words to express my appreciation of what they mean to me. They have walked with me through life's ups and downs and the unimaginable. They have knelt by my office chair, holding my hands. They have wiped away my tears, and in other instances, we've cried together. We have shared countless hugs, and I recall numerous times when they sat quietly across from me at my desk, their loving eyes looking into mine, just listening. Our conversations were and are intentional and always spoken from the heart, whether serious or silly. They have been daily godsends, especially during these past years after Ben's death.

Kathy, another coworker and friend, is another godsend: a beautiful person inside and out. I love the conversations we share. They are always heartfelt; include laughter, tears, and hugs; and cover our favorite topics: spirituality and grandkids! We've also discussed

"Godwinks," and now she and her husband, John—also a coworker—have had their own Godwink experiences. You may be asking, what is a Godwink? For me, it's an experience that offers a blessing at just the right moment: a gift from God. You'll hear me reference such Godwinks throughout my book.

In addition to these amazing people, I work with several others as well. Some may stop by my office to share a story, others come looking for support or needing a pep talk, and some just need a Patti hug. When hardships are mentioned by my colleagues or if they or their loved ones might be facing challenges, I offer to pray for them. When I do, they reciprocate my offer. Regardless of where they are on their journey, it's an opportunity for me to plant seeds of faith and hope.

In addition to talking with my husband and children, I am also in touch with my mom, Ann, typically daily. Mom, now in her 80s, still resides in the country home she and Dad raised us in. While we were not close in my younger years, time has definitely strengthened our bond. We have so much fun spending time together, and I don't take our interactions for granted, having so many friends who've lost their moms at a much younger age. Mom is always up for our next adventure, whether a day trip or overnight excursion! Our joke to each other is "be sure to pack extra underwear" should we add a night to our trip! One of our favorite excursions is staying at Sisters of the Presentation in Dubuque, Iowa, visiting with our friends, Sister Kay and Sister Marie. We love having intentional conversations, receiving their spiritual guidance, sharing time in prayer, and eating the most delicious meals! It's also nice having our private room to go back to and reflect and refuel. I actually spent a lot of time there finalizing this book, which I am so grateful for. Sometimes Terry joins us for these adventures, and other times it's just Mom and me. We never run out of things to talk about or do. It's also been a tremendous blessing watching Mom grow in her faith. I'm so grateful that even at her age, she realizes there is still room for growth and lessons to be learned.

As God would have it, Sister Kay reached out to Terry and me after Ben died. She had read an article about us in Iowa's *Telegraph Herald* and admired our efforts to find goodness by helping others in the wake of losing Ben to suicide. It was through Sister Kay we were introduced to Sister Marie, who hosted numerous grief retreats at King's House in Minnesota over the years. Sister Marie offered us countless resources. They were both blessings from God, and we have been grateful for their friendships ever since. They have been instrumental in our journey.

Another gal pal I love spending time with is Norma. She has been a longtime friend I met at the bank years ago. Even after she moved on and worked for other banks, we stayed in touch and remained great friends, enjoying regular socials. Norma and I used to convene at restaurants but soon realized our servers were ready for us to leave before we were, so now Norma and I meet at my home and enjoy visiting for hours. Norma is truly a blessing and a pillar at the annual BENS Hope event, as is Pam.

My sister, Pam, is two years younger than I, and we chat often as well. Pam provided daycare for Ben, Mandy, and Carrie, and honestly made it doable for me to proceed in my banking career. Who better to love on my kiddos than their Auntie Pam! Obviously, their connection was very special then and over their years growing up. Auntie Pam was always supporting our children. Even after she and Bruce married and had kids of their own, they came to our kids' soccer games, cheering them on from the sidelines. Pam and I have been extremely bonded all our lives. Of course, we experienced growing pains too. But everything happens for a reason, and I know these hardships helped us grow as sisters, as friends, and in our faith.

While the void of Ben's death was felt in our immediate family and was unbearable at times, we witnessed the ripple effect and tremendous impact it had on Pam, Bruce, and their three kids: Derek, Anna, and Dylan. The blessing in this tragic situation is knowing they were and still are there for us and we for them. It was truly a blessing to witness their closeness as cousins and friends, even with a ten-year age difference between our kids and theirs. Derek, their oldest, was probably one of Ben's closest friends and favorite people. Ben and Derek spoke the same language, had a similar sense of humor, loved and knew everything about computers, and enjoyed tearing apart and rebuilding them. Both kind, gentle, and giving souls, they were often off by themselves talking computer jargon. They found comfort, acceptance, and amusement in each other. I know Derek misses Ben terribly. I also know Benjamin loved Derek profusely. Aside from our immediate family, Ben mentioned only Derek in his suicide letter and left him his prized possession: his computer.

After leaving work, I have weekly appointments as well as BENS Hope commitments. That's when the real work begins on my journey of self-discovery and renewal. It began with Alison, my physician's assistant, advising me to get counseling to help deal with the post-traumatic stress disorder I developed after losing Ben. In addition to me seeking counseling, Terry and my daughters were also encouraged to seek counseling. All of us needed support but realized none of us were in a position to offer this to each other at the capacity needed. There is value in talking with someone when you're struggling, expressing the feeling with the issue at hand. When my first counselor experience left me bewildered, our daughter, Carrie, encouraged me to link up with another, Candy, who was her counselor at the time. It was apparent after our first meeting that Candy was the right fit! I recall feeling such a sense of hope and thinking, *Wow, I will survive Ben's death with Candy's help.* I desperately needed and looked forward to our bimonthly meetings as I walked forth on my grief and healing journey. Thank you, Carrie, for connecting me with Candy, another godsend.

Because we hear so many comments from other survivors about counseling, I would like to take this opportunity to share that if the first counselor you meet isn't the right fit, don't be discouraged, but seek other options. These trained professionals can provide tools to help you work through your grief and healing journey, but if you're like me, you prefer feeling a connection to them. If you're unsuccessful at finding a counselor you're comfortable with—which was the case for Terry after a few attempts—or cannot afford counseling, I encourage you to seek support groups in your area or online. Also, please understand it will take more than one visit to get the results you desire. It's a lot of work, but for me, it's also been an investment of time on my grief and healing journey.

Candy also reassured me it was OK to take medication in order to help with how I was feeling. This conversation was an important one since I prefer taking a holistic approach, which I did initially. But as my mind would ruminate hours into the night, I yearned to find solace. After my conversation with Candy, I met with Alison, who discussed options for medications that would best suit me. In some instances, meds may be the answer you or a loved one will need to resort to, whether on a temporary or permanent basis. Taking this step was the answer to one of my prayers, and finally, I was able to get some much-needed rest.

When Candy made the decision to retire early, I was frozen with fear and sadness. I was happy for her, of course, but what about me and moving forward on my grief and healing journey? Candy encouraged me to seek continued counseling from her colleague, Megan. Of course she was right! After my first encounter with Megan, I was confident in proceeding with her. Megan was another godsend, and I am blessed God put her on my path. I have referred a number of survivors to Megan as well. She has offered hope to many on their grief and healing journeys. With Megan's move to a new employer, which impacted our insurance coverage, I had my last session with her. Following Ben's suicide, I spent seven years in counseling.

I recall my final session with Megan, one that was prophetic as she said, "This is God's way of telling you you're ready for the next chapter in life. Let go and let God work through you." And I am trusting this to be true. Of course, I'm not sure how things will work out; I mean, who is? But I will continue keeping my faith in God's plans as I move forward on this journey.

Carrie also introduced me to Tammy, her former boss at UW-Platteville. Tammy was the moderator and helped with the cohesiveness of our family as we initially held bimonthly meetings discussing BENS Hope and our visions for it. I am confident that serving in this capacity was more involved than what Tammy originally thought she signed up for. She also serves as my life coach. Tammy has been my cheerleader and was instrumental in *Tears of Love* coming to fruition. I have the utmost respect and gratitude for all she has done for BENS Hope, my family, and me. Tammy is another godsend in my life.

In addition to working full time and going to coaching and counseling appointments, Terry and I also host monthly Survivors of Suicide (SOS) group meetings as part of our BENS Hope commitments. More is coming on BENS Hope in a later chapter.

Some people have yet to experience an event that is life changing. Maybe you're one of those people? If so, perhaps you would better relate to the global impact of the coronavirus disease, also known as COVID-19. I would imagine for most, we are not the same person we were before the pandemic. Many faced what seemed like insurmountable problems. None of us asked for COVID-19 to happen, but it did whether we liked it or not, and many are still trying to figure out what their new reality looks like because of these circumstances.

Initially, we were given updates from the Centers of Disease Control and Prevention. We were curious about how long we would be wearing masks, practicing social distancing, having to quarantine, going to work, or working remotely from home. We didn't realize how the initial days of COVID-19 would turn into weeks, months, and years. Throughout this time, there was a series of new realities we were faced with: hospitals overflowing with sick people, a shortage of ventilators, people dying, other hospital services postponed. We watched as parents became teachers to their children as schools were shut down. Students and their families had to come to terms with missing out on proms, graduations, musical programs, sporting events, and other school activities. Mandates were enforced for monumental gatherings such as weddings and funerals, adding additional trauma. Many hospitals changed rules with regard to allowing visitors to see patients, and when delivering a child, some gave birth without their partners and were allowed limited, if any, visitors to support them after the birth of their baby. The pandemic affected all sectors of the economy from restaurants, theaters, salons, stores, and warehouses. Businesses across the country saw their supply chains interrupted as we became witnesses to the demand for products but a decline in supplies. I am not sure how COVID-19 has impacted you, whether through challenges or blessings, but whatever your situation may be specifically, I pray it offers opportunities to reflect, prioritize, learn, and grow.

During the COVID-19 pandemic, we held SOS meetings virtually. Witnessing the number of people not only attending within our community, but also those joining us from outside our area and even from across state lines was eye opening. We are grateful BENS Hope is here to offer this much-needed support. If you are dealing or struggling with the aftermath of COVID-19, please seek support by texting HOME to 741741, the Crisis Text Line.

Due to life's struggles all of us go through and realizing we can't carry the burdens on our shoulders alone, Terry and I lean on God's strength. We started attending church again, which is a priority! At one point in our life, our efforts would have been considered "Chreaster" attendances, as we only showed up at Easter and Christmas services. Now we appreciate the significance of being refueled in person every Sunday! We appreciate the difference in attending church because we want to versus out of obligation, as in our earlier years, just because it was expected by others. Just like finding the right therapist, stylist, counselor, etc., we encourage you to seek a church that you are excited to attend! Pastor Mark Dieter offers great Bible teachings and insightful messages and has been instrumental in our faith journey, as have our church families at Bethlehem E&R Church and Lancaster Congregational Church. They are truly beautiful people who we are grateful for. I previously worked on weekends, but that rarely happens now, and if so, not on a Sunday because Sunday is now a day of worship and refueling my soul. Socializing outside of church includes spending time with friends and family, investing in heart-to-heart conversations, eating lunches with my wonderful Fab 5 friends, Gloria, Vicki, Jayne, and, Donna, or texting with my dear friends, Kathy (also known as Reggie) and Becky. Becky and Reg have been my pals since elementary school. I am blessed by these friendships, their love, and their continued support. I enjoy learning about others, supporting them whether they're well known or strangers. That's how God wired me. I am also known for being a good listener and often hear, "Patti, I know I can share this with you without worrying about you repeating it." I appreciate this blessing of trust.

As a mom, I especially adore spending time with my girls. I love to visit Mandy and her dachshund terrier, Olive, our grandpuppy that Mandy rescued from Texas. I relish hearing about her personal chef business (Nourishment—A Personal Chef Service) and watching the progress in her new home. I also cherish time with Carrie, a professional portrait photographer (Carrie Cullen Photography), and Matt and Desiree. Both Desi and Olive have won Terry and me over, and we are grateful for these blessings in life and additions to our family.

In addition to time with our family, we enjoy the great outdoors, another of God's wondrous blessings. Terry and I have always enjoyed spending time in nature, whether biking, camping, glamping, or fishing. We also enjoy time with loved ones around a blazing bonfire or taking in a gentle breeze in the open air.

Throughout the year, Terry and I enjoy trips glamping with Pam and Bruce. While previously Terry and I only tent camped, Pam and Bruce own an RV, and we now get to enjoy it too. Their RV contains all the amenities of home. We enjoy taking adventures to antique and consignment shops, sharing our hearts and stories, and clinking our wine glasses around bonfires. Whether we're watching the vastness of the stars overhead at night or the splendor of God's paintbrush in a sunrise or sunset, we appreciate our time together and all God's blessings.

Those who are wise will shine as bright as the sky, and those who lead
many to righteousness will shine like the stars for ever.
Daniel 12:3 (NLT)

These days, there are few nights when something isn't going on. Since I'm an early riser, once I finish up after work with appointments or other commitments, I'm usually ready for bed. Even as my head hits the pillow, my mind still swirls with thoughts of my son and BENS Hope and how I could—should—will pivot my calling to this next mission. Some might say it's an incredible feat. It's the mission that God and Ben set forth for me. It all started on that one day that changed me and my family forever.

CHAPTER 2

ALL ABOUT BEN

For God so loved the world that He gave His one and only son,
that whoever believes in Him shall not perish but have eternal life.
John 3:16 (NIV)

Out of respect for others who are struggling or have been impacted by suicide, I wish to share in advance that there may be triggering content in the following chapters.

Terry and I were married on September 3, 1983. Terry was 22 and I was 21. We had discussed having children, but the aftermath of losing my brother left me apprehensive about bringing a child into the world and what that might look and feel like. The unknown is scary, and the thought of not being able to protect my child and keep them safe was even scarier. What I was certain of is that I never wanted to again experience the devastating pain I had after losing my brother. The topic of children was further brought to light during our Marriage Encounter prep with Father Bud, our priest at St. Mary's Catholic Church. After he asked us how many children we wanted, Terry's response was seven, while mine was none. I don't recall us answering simultaneously, but I do recall Father's raised eyebrows.

After three years of marriage living in duplex and fourplex housing, and having the conversation and encouragement from Father Bud, we were ready for two things: a house and a baby! We were elated to start our family and experienced the blessing of getting pregnant almost immediately. Finding a house took longer. However, in the city of Platteville, we found a beautiful ranch home complete with a Winnie-the-Pooh nursery, which sealed the deal!

Learning of our pregnancy with Benjamin brought us over-the-moon gratitude and excitement as we eagerly awaited the arrival of our precious child. In addition, it was a new chapter as Terry and I moved out of the rental stage and became new homeowners. Initially during my pregnancy, Terry was very attentive to what I was doing at all times, questioning ingredients I ingested in food or even the type of gum I was chewing. He was very protective of me and our unborn child. I elected to continue walking the mile to work during my pregnancy. While it might not sound like a big deal, it was my first pregnancy, and considering Ben was due in March, I knew full well that the Wisconsin winter would present its challenges. I definitely took precautions by watching my footing to prevent a fall. Getting to work became an art. One day specifically, I recall slipping on ice outside the bank's drive-up window. Fortunately, I fell backward and avoided hitting the ground on my backside by catching myself with my elbows. Whew! That was a close call. While I was a bit shaken, our baby was safe and sound.

Pregnancy was beautiful and also scary with this precious little human growing inside of me. I remember initial concerns of being claustrophobic and experiencing anxiety as I thought about our baby taking up residence in my body. These worries subsided quickly as I focused on our precious little one, bonding more with him every day. My personal favorite experience in pregnancy was feeling our baby's movements. I loved this miraculous experience and still look back with such fond memories of my pregnancies with Ben, Mandy, and Carrie. Each of them was truly a blessing. It's interesting how even in pregnancy I was already thinking about celebrating the milestones ahead and praying all their dreams would come true.

Then a switch went off. The serenity broke when we got the first bill for our mortgage. I witnessed Terry changing and not in a good way. He wasn't the person I married. He became a stranger and made choices that pushed us further apart. This worsened as the baby's due date drew nearer. At times, the pains of loneliness and desperation were completely overwhelming. I recall one specific evening I contemplated going on. This wasn't what I signed up for. At that moment, the baby kicked and reminded me of his presence and that I was not alone. We never know the impact an act can have. I believe being reminded we're not alone is the encouragement we need to move forward.

The situation we found ourselves in was not what others, nor I, expected our lives to be, but I knew the reality that existed behind our closed doors. When family members learned of our circumstances, they attributed everything to my hormones and pregnancy. They weren't there on those nights I was home alone crying or up for hours anxiously awaiting Terry's car pulling into our driveway. My impending motherhood was supposed to be an exciting chapter, right?

A gift from my bank friends at my bridal shower was a large clock inscribed with traditional wedding vows. We hung it prominently on our living room wall. I loved looking at it; it had the same vows Terry and I exchanged on our fairy-tale wedding day. I looked at that clock and recited those vows over and over: "I take you to be my husband, to have and to hold from this day forward, for better, for worse, for richer, for poorer, in sickness and in health, until death do us part." Previously, I apparently focused on the "better, richer, and health" components of our vows, but this clock was a reminder of all the promises Terry and I made to each other. I was there, living the vows we had committed to but on the opposite side of the spectrum of where I wanted to be. I found myself seeking guidance and leaned into my faith.

Commit your way to the Lord; trust in Him, and He will act.
Psalm 37:5 (ESV)

Terry and I went through a rough season in our marriage. By the grace of God, we worked our way through the challenges presented to us and strengthened the foundation of our marriage and faith. Something we've learned during our marriage is that we are both empaths. This has definitely factored into our relationship and taught us to take criticism seriously but not personally. Before we speak, we need to consider: is it true, is it necessary, and is it kind? Many times something is said by one of us and perceived entirely differently by the other. Something that has helped us when this happens is asking the other person, "What did you hear me say?" I have also learned that love isn't just about feelings; it is also about fulfilling the commitment we made to each other the day we exchanged our wedding vows. I am thankful God is always there to see us through these seasons in marriage. For me, it validates that with God all things are possible. Of course, going through that season was a very lonely and difficult time for me, and I don't wish to minimize this. I recall longing for a pill I could take to fast-forward in life and see my destiny ahead to know how this situation would turn out. But that's not how life works, as you probably realize as well. No, we have to endure pains and struggles in life because these experiences offer us valuable lessons and opportunities of growth, whether we're the one going through challenges or witnessing a loved one going through them. Life can be hard, and it definitely doesn't always play fair, but this is life. For anyone reading this who might be going through struggles in their marriage, I pray you are somehow inspired by our story or intrigued by our faith and find hope.

The good news is, Terry was there for Benjamin's birth. I recall when the doctor announced, "It's a boy!" I looked at Terry and said, "You have a son." It would be the only time Terry would hear these words that he held close to his heart then and will forever. Benjamin was born on March 5, 1987, at 2:55 a.m., weighing in at 7 pounds 4 ounces and measuring 20 inches. While this information may not matter to everyone, it's typically a mom's pleasure to share these details since most do take interest! Benjamin Richard, his middle name given in honor of my dad, had a full head of dark hair and deep blue eyes. Immediately, I noticed how big Ben's feet and hands were in proportion to his body. Interestingly enough, I noticed these same features on our grandbaby, Desi. It must run in the family! Benjamin was perfect in every way. For anyone who has yet to discover love at first sight, this was the case for me when Benjamin was born, and again with Mandy and Carrie. Seeing your child for the first time offers a love like no other; it's hard to explain but easy to understand once you're holding your baby in your arms. I celebrate with those of you who have had this experience and pray for those of you who await it.

As exciting as it was to bring Benjamin into the world, Terry and I separated a few months later after an altercation. I personally struggled with embarrassment and humiliation about our separation. I had this overwhelming sense of shame about my marriage not working, so much that it prevented me from taking Ben to the nursing home to meet my maternal grandma, Mary. To this day, I regret not visiting Grandma and introducing her to my newborn son. Looking back, I wonder what would happen if we allowed others to see our vulnerability? Why can't we be honest about our feelings and truthful when we're suffering? Why should we hold the guilt that we're letting others down because of our present circumstances? When we are down, why shouldn't we seek or accept support from others? How do they know of our sadness or despair if we work so hard to cover it up? I share this so that you realize it is OK not to be OK. Seek support. It's not a sign of weakness but a sign of strength.

I definitely appreciate and share my emotions more freely now than I ever have in my lifetime. I understand the benefits of being truthful about my feelings. In turn, I've noticed that my being honest and vulnerable with others serves as an invitation for them to trust and feel safe sharing their thoughts and feelings with me. It has been a beautiful experience to witness the blessings that accompany sharing brokenness and hurt and finding peace, love, and support in difficult circumstances.

Benjamin was a very snuggly, easy-going, mild-mannered, sweet baby boy, and his kind and gentle nature stayed with him through his toddler years. His demeanor encouraged us to have more children. We've shared over the years that it is a good thing Ben was born first! Benjamin loved Bert and Ernie on *Sesame Street* when he was little and later loved *Thomas the Tank Engine & Friends*! His bed sheets, birthday cakes, and toy box validated this. That is, until he discovered *Teenage Mutant Ninja Turtles*! They became his new favorite! I recall Ben dressing up as a ninja, which was quite entertaining. Ben enjoyed building things and tearing them apart, which would play into his passion for computers later in life, but in his younger years, his passion was Legos. He had tons of Lego sets! We saved them for our grandkids to enjoy.

At the ripe age of 15 months old, Benjamin was promoted to a big brother! He was still a baby himself. I recall looking down the hallway of the hospital as Terry and Benjamin approached my room the day after my second delivery. My heart felt *so much* love seeing my precious little man toddling down toward me with Daddy in hand next to him. If I'm being honest, I was a little overwhelmed with emotions. Just the night before, Benjamin had been our baby boy, and now, a day later, he was promoted to big brother. Of course, we were all elated as we welcomed our newest addition and blessing from God, Amanda Lynn Marie.

I would like to take this moment to share with those having another child who have any doubts or concerns that I learned quickly it *is* possible to love your next child as much as you love your first. So for anyone reading this and wondering, please let me reiterate, yes! It is possible, and you will have as much love for the next baby and the next and so on. God blesses us with tremendous abilities to love unconditionally and massively! When the umbilical cord is cut, God ensures this love remains strong, whether through loving our child in this lifetime on earth or in their death.

We welcomed Amanda "Mandy" into our lives on June 27. Mandy was the first granddaughter on my side of the family, which was a pretty big deal! I often share that Terry and I blessed my parents with their first granddaughter, and it was one of the biggest accomplishments of my life! Thank you, Lord! It's truly a blessing how Mandy's arrival brought our family back together. Her birth encouraged opportunities to offer forgiveness and heal from hurts that occurred the previous year. Of course we don't forget these tough experiences, but we can absolutely grow from them, if we choose to, and move forward in life. Mandy was born on the eve of my grandma Mary's birthday. I took this as a sign and Godwink from God.

Two years later, Ben would be promoted again, as would Mandy, when their baby sister joined the world June 28. That's right! I was in labor with baby No. 3 on Mandy's 2nd birthday. When I got home from work, we had enough time to put a candle in a brownie, sing "Happy Birthday" to Mandy, and head to Mercy Hospital in Dubuque! Auntie Pam stayed with Ben and Mandy while Terry and I made the trip to the hospital to bring our third greatest blessing into the world, our brown-eyed, red-haired baby girl, Carrie Ann. Readers, did you catch the Godwink here? Remember, Mandy was born on the eve of my grandma's birthday, and two years later, Carrie was born on my grandma Mary's birthday! A coincidence? I think not! Definitely a Godwink for me.

Ben, Mandy, and Carrie were great playmates for each other and lots of fun for us, as any parent can imagine. But as we know, with kids also comes lots of work. We had crazy-busy days and experienced many disrupted nights of sleep. As I write this, I reflect on all the nights of musical beds—but we did what we needed to get our sleep before tackling the day ahead and starting this process all over again.

We enjoyed our evenings, whether playing hide-and-go-seek, going for bike rides or going to the library, climbing the Big M, walking along the water path at the UW-P, having bathtub time with lots of bubbles, having story time, or making a special trip on Monday nights to McDonald's for burgers. Many times we weren't sure what end was up in our household, but thankfully, Auntie Pam and Terry's sister, their Aunt Connie, spent *lots* of time at our home helping out. Pam and Connie were an extended part of our family and built-in helpers, entertaining kids, bathing them, or working on laundry. It didn't matter what we needed, they were here to help! We appreciated all of their contributions, enjoyed their company and conversations, and most importantly, welcomed their support and love for our family. While there were moments I wondered what we got ourselves into having three kids within four years as Terry and I held full-time jobs outside our home, we appreciated the blessing of our children. I recall sharing with others on multiple occasions that getting home after work and seeing our kiddos was like having Christmas every day! I loved pulling in and seeing their little noses pressed up against the windows, peeking out and anxiously awaiting my arrival. As I entered, they would leap into my arms, receiving an abundance of hugs and kisses. These are moments I will cherish in my heart forever. I reassured Terry over the years countless times that our kids are definitely our best investments in life and our greatest blessings from God.

Happy memories surrounded our Christmas traditions, which started with our family trotting off into the wilderness, typically around Thanksgiving, and cutting down a pine tree. This was accomplished initially on the property of Terry's folks' family farm. Together, we would cut down a pine tree that Terry would reassure us would "green up." But it never did, and it quite honestly didn't matter, because once the lights were put on our tree, it was always perfect! I recall one year, after taking our kiddos out for this holiday excursion, hearing gunshots off in the distance. Terry shared that November was also deer hunting season, so we changed a few things for the safety of everyone involved. We now visit Christmas tree farms only. We are grateful our kids have carried on this family Christmas tree tradition as well.

Another tradition was having each of the kids receive a gift in their Christmas stocking. Ben's Christmas stocking always contained a small Lego set. He was always the first one up in the early, wee hours of the morning. Of course, Ben watched out for his sisters, so he made sure to let Mandy and Carrie know Santa had visited! Ben would then proceed to put his Lego set together and was excited to share it with us when we got up. Ben also loved trains. I mean, he really loved them! I can't recall the number of train sets he received over the years, but there were *lots!* In later years, Ben also loved assisting Santa by putting out gifts. This worked nicely since Ben was a night owl. In the morning, we just savored spending family time together. Their presence was the only gift I always requested; it was the best present I could ever receive. It still is.

Benjamin was considerate of his sisters and watched out for them in their childhood and adulthood too. I recall instances when the girls would have friends over and Ben was attentive to them as well. A couple of memories that come to mind are from when the girls had sleepovers. I recall Ben baking a frozen pizza, leaving it by their bedroom door, knocking, and then sneaking away. That was the thing about Ben, he didn't do things for notoriety; he was just a kind person. Another time, I recall Ben hauling the mattress from his bedroom into the family room so the girls' friends who didn't get dibs on the recliner or sleeper sofa would have the comfort of his mattress versus the sleeping bags on the floor. Ben's kindness as a child definitely carried over into his adulthood. He seemed to put others before himself and was aware of their needs or what he thought they needed. He was caring and considerate, a definite empath.

In addition to going to Pam's for daycare, Ben attended preschool. We loved attending his programs and watching his interactions with his preschool friends. At home, Ben enjoyed time on the swing set and sandbox in our backyard and also cruised around on his battery-operated Power Wheels, which I might add, have come a long way since his childhood! Our kids took private swimming lessons, and we learned from their instructor that Ben was a natural at it! At that time, community lessons weren't offered after work, nor were all the programs in school. Ben also participated in summer recreational activities, attended church camp, enjoyed bike rides, and hung with his friends. Terry recalls a time when Ben was younger and he and his buddies, Scott and Caleb, were caught using a magnifying glass with plastic toy soldiers and ants as their victims. The things those boys came up with!

I recall moments in Ben's life that were exceptionally challenging for him. One was being diagnosed in elementary school with attention-deficit disorder (ADD). Typical symptoms included a short attention span, difficulty listening, and impulsivity. I'm not a doctor, but I questioned his short attention span. Ben played with Lego sets for hours and later would game or work on a computer for hours. And Ben seemed to understand and follow directions just fine. One question he did ask daily when he was very young was, "Is today tomorrow?" Maybe there was more to this confusing statement, but at the time, we just found it adorable! We trusted those at school had Ben's best interest at heart and listened to a new, young teacher diagnose our son before sending us to a doctor known for their pill pushing. His diagnosis of ADD followed Ben through high school and even required him to attend two learning disability (LD) classes.

I appreciated the help that was made available and provided to Ben, and I am not discounting these services whatsoever. Honestly, I feel ADD is better known and understood today, unlike it was back then. I questioned this diagnosis often because through the following years and high school, there were multiple teachers, including his LD teachers, who shared that Ben did not have ADD, nor should he be in those classes. Interestingly enough, after Ben passed, Terry and I received counseling support from a psychiatrist who shared that many kids were actually misdiagnosed with ADD when, in essence, they needed glasses. I have read research since then to support this, and Ben did end up getting glasses. Regardless, that was the road we traveled with our son. I encourage you to advocate for your child as we believe we missed this opportunity with Ben.

Ben also served as an altar boy at the Catholic church we attended and made all the sacraments as recognized by the Catholic Church. As parents, neither Terry nor I questioned our church or faith. And as parents, we didn't question our children either. We only introduced them to what we knew and what was passed down from generations before. What I have learned since is not to get stuck on religion but to find a relationship with the Creator. It can be life-changing, and for me personally, my faith in God saved my life.

In his youth, Ben played recreational soccer, and then his interest reemerged again in high school. While most of the team had been playing soccer together for years, Ben had not. He started out on the junior varsity (JV) team and got a lot of playing time. As he built endurance and sharpened his techniques, Ben's teammates realized his potential and the asset he was to their team. Ben played left defense, and besides having extreme speed, he was also ambidextrous! It was exhilarating to watch Ben and his teammates play soccer. We were always in the crowd and highly anticipated each upcoming game! Seriously, it was one of our favorite pastimes. Ben, Jesse—Mandy's then high school sweetheart—along with Scottie, Caleb, and so many others made the sport memorable, all of them giving 100 percent in each game! It was exhilarating! I imagine their bodies are feeling it by now. I know Mandy has commented multiple times that her body does, but she still continues to be active in sports. She is a competitor!

The following year, when Ben was a sophomore, he again tried out for the varsity team but did not make the cut. I imagine Coach Matt envisioned Ben getting more playing time on JV and continued opportunities to sharpen his skills, but regardless of the reasoning, Ben was devastated! It was one of the few times I witnessed Ben cry. I was at Pam's for a Pampered Chef party when Ben unexpectedly showed up at her front door. It was apparent he was upset. It was unusual to see Ben vulnerable. I was caught off guard by his behavior and played down his feelings rather than validating them. I reassured Benjamin of the opportunities he would have on the JV team. I also reminded Ben he could try out for the varsity team again the next season. While I felt good about our conversation, I now believe as Ben's mom that it was another missed opportunity. I don't feel I fulfilled the need Ben had or offered the support he desired. I've learned since then that when a guy talks, *put things down, pay attention, and listen!* Just listen. We learned this while offering support to students on campus at UW-Platteville. A frequent comment these kids shared was they don't want their parents to try and fix their situation for them, they just want to be heard by them. And just because they were honest with their parents about their struggles, they didn't need them to become helicopter parents; they just needed their support. I wish I had listened to what Ben was saying and validated his feelings rather than trying to fix the situation. As a parent, it's a reaction I typically had and sometimes still do. I want to fix the situation so my children don't have to deal with or feel their pain, hurt, or disappointment. Looking back, I see what a disservice this was to my kids. I needed to allow them to grow and see the world as it was and the life that would come their way. Ben was really pouring himself out to me, but I didn't listen to what he was saying or interpret the magnitude of what he was feeling. I still deeply regret this. I pray you won't miss out on such opportunities like I did.

Speaking of soccer, I recall one of the games Ben was playing in when he got hit hard. I noticed him holding his wrist a bit, but he played through the remainder of the game. It wasn't until afterward he shared the pain he was in, and after taking him to the doctor, we learned his hand was broken. Ben never drew attention to himself or wanted to be a bother. It was incredible the pain he appeared to tolerate. Looking back, it makes me question how many other times Ben was tolerating pain, in silence, alone. I question how many of you reading this right now may be tolerating pain in silence and feeling alone. If so, I ask that you please reach out for help. You are not alone. You matter, you are wonderful, and you were made for a purpose. I pray you stay and fulfill your greater purpose.

The LORD has made everything for its purpose.
Proverbs 16:4a (ESV)

When our kids were younger, we encouraged them to get jobs during the summer. Our friend and neighbor, Mary Kay, enlisted her daughter, Katie, and son, Caleb, to work for Golden Harvest. Our kids also worked there. Because they didn't have their driver's licenses yet, as parents, we were responsible for getting them to and from Golden Harvest. The kids spent their days pollinating corn in the fields with access to a porta potty and water to keep them hydrated under the hot summer sun. Our hope was they wouldn't get sunburned or pass out in the heat. That lasted a couple of summers until Ben suffered from heat exhaustion. That incident ended their time at Golden Harvest.

While working on this chapter about Ben, I had the pleasure of reaching out to others and inquiring about their interest in sharing memories to offer you, the reader, additional insight to get a better idea of who Ben was. What a blessing to hear from those who responded! I wish to extend a sincere thank you to those who took the time to contribute to this chapter and for offering kindness, love, and friendship to Ben.

First you'll hear from my mom, Ann:

> Ben was my fourth grandchild and my fourth grandson. I love to spoil, as grandparents often do. Ben was the sweetest young fellow and always so polite and loving. We read the Beatrix Potter stories of Peter Rabbit and Benjamin Bunny when he stayed overnight, which was often. We read and reread them, as I think it was a way for him to keep from having to sleep or to see who would fall asleep first, he or Grandma!

> We spent a lot of time at the campground in the camper and at the pool, which were fun outdoor summertime activities for all. I loved going to all his soccer games from young on and going to all the school activities we were invited to.

As he grew and gained all of his knowledge, he became my IT fellow to go to, and he took care of all my computer, printer, and internet questions and any problems I got myself into. He purchased a printer for me one Christmas that just decided this last summer to no longer work. One day, I lost pages of information for my taxes and called him. He told me, "Gram, give me ten minutes." I loved watching the phantom arrow move across my computer screen. That was Ben connecting to my computer as he fixed my problem from long distance. He was so knowledgeable and built computers and did not buy them ready-made. I guess there were always parts he could add to his liking.

What a fine man he was, and we were so proud of him and all of his accomplishments. I looked forward to a great future for him.

It broke my heart to have him make the decision to not to be here with us any longer, a decision he had to have been planning for a long time and then carried out. What a hurt he has left us to live with. I love you, Ben.

Here's a story from Ben's friend, Scott, a friend since childhood.

Ben, Caleb, and I were young and dumb kids at the time and in fifth or sixth grade. I recall a storm/flood overflow channel at the south end of Miners Field (a soccer field kids used to compete at), and during heavy rain storms, which happened all the time in the summer, the flood channel filled with gushing water flowing almost as fast as rapids. We thought we were invincible, as many kids do, and thought it would be fun to try and run down the hill and jump over the gushing water channel. As an adult, I now realize how dumb and dangerous it was, because if we hadn't landed the jump—which we almost didn't several times—we would have been swept away down the flood channel that led underneath North Washington Street and may not have survived. We jumped over a five- to six-foot gap of gushing water in the middle of the pouring rain while thunder and lightning was overhead.

Scott admitted to me that I am the first parent to hear this story. I appreciate you, Scott, for sharing this, and I thank God for keeping the boys safe during their young adventurous years of taking such risks.

Next is an excerpt from Ben's best friend since childhood, Caleb:

Not many people get to grow up across the street from their best friend, work at three same places of employment, and live together for years.

Ben was always there for the people in his life when they needed anything. He was a smart, positive, thoughtful, and empathetic human. He was also the best problem solver of technical issues I have ever met. He taught me so many skills that are still part of my identity in life to this day. I believe he knew that I appreciated his friendship because I told him frequently. I can only hope he knows that he was more of a brother than just a best friend to me and that I would have done anything for him. We were both pretty quiet, introverted people and were not the best at expressing our emotions to others. On the occasions I would open up to him or vent about my problems, he would always try to make me feel better and distract me from them. I thought I had done the same for him. I just wish I was more open emotionally and asked him how he was doing more often. Ben was an amazing human, and his memory lives on through each and every person that met him. I truly believe everyone that knew him feels the same. I am thankful and am a better person for the time I got to have him in my life.

When we lived together, we had an unforgettable telescope adventure at Apple Blossom Bluffs in La Crescent, Minnesota:

Ben asked me if I wanted to do some stargazing with him up on the bluffs. It was a few days before a full moon, the skies were clear, and he really wanted to use his new light filters for his Orion SkyQuest XT8 Classic Dobsonian Telescope. We packed up some snacks and drinks and loaded the telescope and lawn chair into his Honda Civic. On our way, while driving through downtown La Crosse, we were pulled over for no reason. The two officers that pulled us over suspiciously and aggressively asked us where we were going and about the giant bag that took up the entire back seat. Ben told them it was a telescope, and they asked what kind of telescope is that big. Without missing a beat, Ben told them it was an Orion large aperture Classic Dobsonian Reflector Telescope, the stand was in the trunk, it was the perfect time of year to view the planet Jupiter and its major moons, and that we were heading up to the bluffs to get away from the light pollution of the city. After hearing this and looking at us, the officers kind of laughed and said we could go. We figured that they were probably looking for drunk drivers downtown on a Saturday night.

Finally, we arrived at the bluffs and parked on a big gravel shoulder of the road. Maybe five minutes later, two police officers parked about fifty feet from us and came over. While walking over to us, they both had a flashlight in one hand and the other on their holster. They yelled, asking what we were doing. To add some perspective, this is not a normal-looking telescope that most people think of. It is a four- to five-foot long tube that is about a foot wide in diameter and sitting on a rotating base, so to them I guess it probably looked like a cannon or some kind of mortar launcher set up next to us.

After realizing it was a telescope, I remember their attitude toward us changed. Ben asked one of the officers if they wanted to look at the moon. After seeing the amazing detail of the craters on the moon, the officer's mind was blown, and he got the other officer to look as well. They stayed for about an hour and actually ended up calling their wives to tell them about it while we were all hanging out and laughing. Ben went into detail, answering questions about constellations and even showing them some of the moons of Jupiter.

From my time spent working with Ben at Kaplan:

Wendy hired me at Kaplan entirely because of Ben's recommendation. I thanked him so many times for getting me a job at Kaplan. It honestly got to the point where he told me he got it and to stop mentioning it, and then we would laugh a bit.

We once worked 45-plus days straight together. He was training me at work to get me up to speed so I could make some extra money. We both signed up to answer weekend emails for almost two months since nobody else wanted to. We would just play video games with work-email breaks every weekend. We had 50 to 50-plus hour workweeks.

On top of having an amazing work ethic and being loved by everyone at work, Ben was known all around the office for being a wizard with computers and technology. Coworkers were always dropping off their laptops or scheduling a house call to fix their home computer/internet/printer issues. Multiple nights every week after work he would spend some time either working on someone's old laptop, recovering photographs from a broken computer, or reimaging or fixing a computer. In most cases, they were laptops. He also became very well known for his cheesy potato recipe (I think a family recipe) he made for all of the potlucks at work. It was always gone before everything else. I carpooled with him a lot when I was having constant car problems too.

Thank you, Caleb, for contributing to Ben's life and sharing these memories. I appreciate hearing old stories again and hearing others for the first time. It does sadden me to think that you were the one who had to find Ben after he took his life. As devastating as it was, I feel like Ben knew you might understand and forgive him. I hope you have forgiven yourself for any guilt you might be holding on to because of Ben's death, Caleb. You were one of his best friends, and he loved you like a brother.

As fondly shared by Wendy, who hired Ben at Kaplan in La Crosse:

> I think about Ben and your family often. I always remember Ben and his sweet smile. When he had his interview to work at Kaplan for technical support, he didn't have much work experience. But when he told me about his love for computers and how he would take them apart and rebuild them, he pretty much won me over and was hired on the spot! Ben was very good at his job and was liked by both customers and his coworkers. After Ben was there a few months, I asked him if he had any other friends like him who might be interested in working at Kaplan. That's when Caleb joined Kaplan, and then later Travis was also hired. Ben had great talent and a bright future. I actually still have his name and phone number in my cell. I can't bring myself to delete it.

Terry and I first met Wendy when Ben took us to Kaplan over a weekend we were visiting in La Crosse. He proudly showed us around his new stomping grounds! We were impressed with the aesthetics of the Kaplan building, inside and out, and the fact that it sat on a beautiful waterfront enhanced its beauty and our experience! We were happy for Ben and so proud of him. It was apparent he was pleased as well. Wendy was on-site, so of course Ben introduced us to her. Wendy shared with us how Ben was so kind and "such a great worker." Talk about first impressions! We were delighted when Wendy continued, saying, "I would be pleased if I could raise my boys with half the kindness Ben offers." If only the world would treat others the way parents desire others would treat their children. Thank you, Wendy, for loving our Ben. We know he considered you as his "work mom," and you meant the world to him and us.

Another memory Wendy and I shared was when Ben gave up his technical support position to an older gentleman. Ben was hesitant to move up to the next level of IT, but by doing so, ensured the older gentleman kept his employment. Wendy knew Ben was more than ready for the promotion, and she knew best.

Kaplan was not only Ben's employer, it also served as a place for him to advance his education. In addition to the countless hours he put into work, Ben was committed to taking classes to attain his bachelor's degree. I was so proud of his determination to accomplish this goal. Ben also shared his computer knowledge by assisting others who needed help with their computers, whether on the job or outside of work. I remember referring a couple of my coworkers to Ben when they were in the market for a new computer. Ben took the time to ask questions about what they were seeking in a computer, did the market research, helped them pick the computer that best suited their needs, and then even volunteered to set it up for them when it arrived. That was Ben: so gracious, so kind, so selfless.

Another contributor was Asha, Vice President of Student Services, who was Ben's friend and coworker at Kaplan:

> Ben was the kind of man who made you feel more comfortable just by being in the same room as him. He had an innate call that was contagious; he gave you the freedom to be who you are, have a bad day, share a hard time. He was an incredible listener, hard worker, and loyal friend. His kindness is what I remember most, along with his ability to come up with solutions out of thin air due to his intellect, all combined with a genuine humility.

Thank you, Asha, for your kindness, love, support, and prayers for Ben then and since his death. You were a blessing to Ben and are a continued blessing to us.

Ben was promoted three times during his five-year career at Kaplan. He had so many success stories and so much potential. Unfortunately, Ben made the lone decision to take his life before he could see how his story and future accomplishments would unfold. We'll never know how his life could have played out. It's heartbreaking. We live with the reality of what will never be.

Below is another fond remembrance from Ben's best friend, Mark:

I know there are many, many, many stories that I could share about Ben. He was one of my two best friends. I was fortunate to spend a lot of time with Ben, and unfortunately, the pain has not gotten better. I hope that these stories can help bring some joy to those who knew Ben and have lost a loved one.

One story is of the night of his 21st birthday. The unfortunate part of the story was his girlfriend broke up with him. I was the only one who was 21 at that time, and Ben asked me to take him downtown to get drunk, as he was having a rough start to his birthday. We went to several different bars, and they each gave him a free drink. After a while, he was thoroughly drunk. We were leaving the last bar when Ben said, "Mark, that door is soooooo big, you have to open it for me!" The best part after that was getting home and the fact that everything was covered in ice. Ben held on to me as we walked back to the car, slipping and almost falling every few steps. We got back, and there were plenty of large snowbanks on the side of the road. Ben went to get out of the car, fell into a snowbank, and was unable to get up. He started yelling for help as he just couldn't get up. After I finished laughing, I helped him up and got him into the house, where he was quite loud.

Some of the funniest stories involve doing stupid things while out at the cabin. There was a time when Ben tipped the ATV over into the creek while Dan Hamilton was riding on the back. It was a trip we made all the time, and there were two different levels. He went from the upper to the lower when the steering wheel caught and took them right toward the creek. He tried to correct and tipped in sideways. Later that weekend, my dad asked how the headlight was bent down, and we lied and said we had no idea.

We had lots of fun at the cabin shooting clay pigeons. We did this pretty regularly over the summers. Ben would bring his dad's 20-gauge, and I would have my dad's. Ben was always the one to coordinate these get-togethers. He would contact everyone and invite them to the cabin. Prior to Ben's passing, we had stocked up on clay pigeons and had the shotgun shells ready for the next time. Unfortunately, that never happened. The pigeons remain in our shed at the cabin, and I am unable to bring myself to throw them out, even though they are no longer good.

There's also a story about my wedding and time on the cruise ship. I was only part of this story for half of it. We had our shore excursion where it was all-you-could-eat-and-drink. I was drunk, my wife was sober, and Ben was very drunk. Ben asked if we could take him with us back to the cruise ship, which of course we did. Later on while hanging out, Brandon—a groomsman—stated he went back to his room and Ben was naked on top of his covers, and he stayed that way for many hours until he woke up.

We had many other great times together, like the time at Wisconsin Dells and driving to Dubuque at midnight to get Wendy's. Then there was the time I took him out and we went deer hunting. The loss of Ben and then Brandon has changed a lot of what I find enjoyment in. I lost interest in games that Ben and I played together, such as World of Warcraft, Command & Conquer, and many others.

I have avoided most of the things surrounding Ben, as I am not ready yet: the SOS group, the BENS Hope walks, etc. It is not because I do not care, as that couldn't be further from the truth. I am still trying to come to terms with him being gone. I mean, I can't even throw out the rotted clay pigeons at our cabin. Aside from my wife, at the time, he was the person I spent the most time with.

Thank you, Mark, for sharing this. I know you have so many memories of Ben, and it's hard to dig deep into the well of them because when we do, it brings pain and sadness, but we also pray it brings memories of laughter and happiness from some of the crazy stuff you enjoyed as well. Thank you for being a best friend to Ben and sharing your life, love, and all your incredible adventures, especially at your family's cabin. Ben loved being there with you and the guys, and Ben loved you, Mark. Please remember that.

Mark's story was entertaining to me because while Benjamin would on occasion have an apple cider beer, he was better known for being the designated driver, especially when he got a call from his sisters. Mark's story validates one of the many coping mechanisms we may resort to in order to deal with our pain or struggles. Unfortunately, alcohol is a depressant, so while it may help you find temporary relief from the challenges in life, tomorrow will still come, and the reality of whatever needs to be worked through will still be there. Trust me, I know this all too well from my personal experiences, especially after losing my brother in 1981. Alcohol was a crutch for sure.

I also received a response from Jesse, Mandy's high school sweetheart who spent so much time at our house. Jesse and his fiancé, Theresa, and daughter, Joyce, recently moved to the Carolinas. When Jesse received my message, he replied by saying the timing of my message was incredible. The transition of this move from Wisconsin to the Carolinas had been very difficult. He was missing Wisconsin badly. He told me about his job as an Amazon driver and the treacherous roads he travels on a daily basis. Doing his deliveries also means parking and going on foot to places he's not familiar with. When he opened my message, he said he sat down and wept. It literally made him pause and put things in his life in perspective. Jesse told me that he and Ben had an unspoken love, and he didn't realize how much this relationship meant to him until after Ben's death. My message brought out so many emotions for him. Thank you, Jesse, for sharing about the perfect timing of my message and the impact Ben's life had on you. You'll always be a part of our family.

Another challenge for Ben was experiencing a breakup. I am confident that anyone who has gone through a breakup or may currently be going through one can relate. Breakups are devastating, especially if the breakup wasn't your idea. Ben was no different; breakups were difficult. I recall Ben's first breakup with Tessa, his first love. Tessa was introduced to Ben through his friends. She lived in a nearby community, about a thirty-minute drive from Platteville. Tessa was a freshman, I believe, when they started dating, and Ben was a senior. Tessa was a sweetheart but definitely bashful. We welcomed her with open arms and witnessed their relationship grow from friendship to love. They adored each other. As time went on, I allowed my kids' significant others to sleep over. However, I did not support them sleeping together. Between Tessa's overnight stays and Mandy's high school boyfriend Jesse's visits, our family dinners served seven instead of five. And as their mom, I had to keep a watchful eye out! My concerns grew when I learned Tessa's age and that she was younger than Ben. The last thing I wanted was for Tessa to become pregnant and Benjamin, being over 18, becoming charged with a statutory rape and landing in jail. After having countless conversations with our kids about saving yourself for marriage, my conversations shifted to "you better make sure you're using protection," which was a pretty big deal coming from this old-fashioned mom. I recall gasping when condoms fell from Ben's pants pocket as I was putting his jeans into the washing machine. I eventually had to come to terms with this reality and accept they were taking precautions. That was a big pill for me to swallow.

We hit an exciting milestone when Benjamin graduated from high school. We celebrated with a graduation party and invited all of our family and friends! He appreciated everyone who attended to share in this milestone. Ben was especially flattered to see his boss from TC Networks attend. Ben had spent his senior year in a co-op program that offered him work in his field of passion: computers. He gained a paycheck and the ability to leave school early each day. He loved this! We were so happy for Ben and proud of his accomplishments as well as grateful for TC Networks believing in him and giving him this opportunity.

 Since Ben's death, I recall a Godwink involving TC Networks on Ben's Angelversary. I was on my way to work, and a truck at an intersection legally turned right as I waited for the stoplight to turn green. I proceeded through the intersection and followed the vehicle as it took the next two lefts, heading the same direction I was going. As I got out of my vehicle and gazed at the stopped truck, I saw TC Networks inscribed on the side of the vehicle. I was thankful for this 2020 Godwink, a hello from heaven.

After high school, and with three scholarships in hand, Ben started college at Southwest Technical College in Fennimore, Wisconsin. He elected to live at home and drive the sixty-minute round trip commute versus living in the dorms offered on campus. We were excited about this next chapter in Ben's life. When Ben wasn't at school, he seemed to be gaming, driving around in his Jeep, or hanging out with his friends. College was not a topic of discussion Ben would engage in, and I would eventually understand why. It was during Ben's second semester of college when I elected to join Ben's advisor meeting. Ben was extremely quiet on the ride over. Any guesses why? Well, you see, it was at this meeting I learned that Ben had not been showing up for classes. Interestingly enough, Terry had suspected this, having seen Ben driving around town. But as Ben's mom, of course I gave him the benefit of the doubt and denied this accusation. Ben came clean after the advisor meeting and shared that he decided college wasn't his thing. He had withheld this secret for fear of judgment and disappointing us and others. I wish he would have just been honest. I know as parents we want the best for our children, but what I have learned is that what we desire for them may not be what they desire for themselves. Happiness on both sides can look differently, and that's OK. It's taken a lot of time to accept this realization, but if my insight is helpful to you, then I am thankful for saving you time, energy, and money. Once

Ben felt he was in the clear, rather than spending his time at school or work, we noticed he was enjoying time on the computer, hanging with friends, rebuilding computers, or gaming. Gaming was Ben's thing! Gaming is a big thing for a lot of people. To remedy this, I owned a women's exercise studio at the time and informed Ben that if he didn't get a job soon, he would become an employee for me. Needless to say, this suggestion did not go over well.

During Ben's lull from college, Tessa spent most of her time at our place. I, rather than Ben, was the one interacting with her while he was off gaming, hanging with friends, or staying at his second home at Caleb's across the street. While I loved Tessa profusely, I questioned her being a priority in Ben's life. I think Ben enjoyed knowing Tessa was around. He knew he wasn't investing much time in her, but of course, I was. Honestly, I'm not sure what a loving relationship looked like to Tessa since she didn't bring this to Ben's attention herself. Maybe she just enjoyed the love, safety, and family environment our home offered. I did talk with Ben about their relationship on more than one occasion, but it seemed to fall on deaf ears. And I wanted Ben to understand that our idea of him growing up and graduating meant more than being an adult, living downstairs, and gaming. He eventually started working, which we were thankful for. I guess we thought Ben needed a wake-up call, or at least, that's how strongly we felt about the situation at the time. Since Ben's death, I have wondered multiple times where his life would be if I kept my nose out of it, if he would still be here. Obviously, I don't know. What I do know is that Terry and I did our best as parents with what we knew at the time.

After Tessa broke up with Ben, he struggled in his work and home life. I really didn't think too much of it at the time, but I did notice a change in his behavior. I recall waking up in bed one morning and seeing Ben standing next to me with such a sad look on his face. He was beside himself, so distraught. He startled me, and I think that was more of my focus rather than what was on his heart. I recall another instance when I was at Walmart shopping. Ben was working there at the time, and he appeared right behind me all of a sudden, which freaked me out. He was actually a broken-hearted young man, confused, sad, and desperately searching for answers and wanting relief from this unfamiliar pain he had never experienced before. I wish I had paid more attention to Ben's feelings and been more sympathetic when he was hurting so badly.

Feelings of pain and sadness are agonizing to work through. I have experienced breakups and survived, as have Mandy and Carrie, so I just assumed it was Ben's turn and that he would figure it out and be OK too. As difficult as it is to see our kids struggle, I realize these "growing pains" are opportunities for extreme personal growth. Looking back now and considering Ben's actions, I realize he was attempting to reach out. I would handle this situation differently if given another chance. First, I would listen, really listen to hear what he's saying, then validate his feelings, ask how I can best offer support, and find support for him through counseling if needed. Obviously, I won't get this chance, but maybe you will.

As I reflect on these crucial moments in Ben's life, I realize I didn't check in with my son like he needed me to. I remember thinking someone needs to write a book about helping your child survive going through a breakup. Interestingly enough, here I am, addressing breakups in this book and sharing insight based on real-life experiences.

Since Ben's death, Terry and I have been part of numerous conversations where others have linked their loved ones' suicide to a breakup. I am not saying this to alarm anyone or suggest that your loved ones' breakup will end with a suicide. Please understand that is not my intention whatsoever. I am sharing that on my personal journey, I have had many, many conversations with people who've lost loved ones to suicide and believe that relationships contributed to their loved ones' decisions to take their lives. Maybe it was the final drip in a cup that finally ran over. Our threshold for emotional pain can only withstand so much, right?

Another insight is with regard to having a loved one in a marriage or relationship that is strained or on the brink of divorce. From the stories shared, their loved one is usually struggling desperately and trying with all their heart to make their relationship work while their partner is not. Sound familiar? Maybe it feels relatable to you as you're reading this book. It's understandable that family members will have ill feelings toward the significant other hurting their family member. But it seems the family becomes so engrossed in what the significant other is doing wrong, they forget to ask their loved one how they are doing. I question the energy and time wasted on the significant other that could be better spent invested in their loved one. I would think such focus would increase the anxiety and amplify the stress for the family member who is already struggling. I only wish that our loved ones contemplating suicide in a broken relationship would understand that the person they wished loved them will not be affected by their suicide the way they want them to be. The ones that will be are those who genuinely love and care about them, and their decision of suicide will impact their loved ones for the rest of their lives on this earth. My encouragement for those trying to help a loved one struggling is to give your love, energy, and time to them. Focus on their needs. Ask how they're dealing with their circumstances and how you can best support them. Be sure to check in. Be proactive instead of reactive. Don't live with regret. Please have the tough conversation versus looking back and wishing you had.

Something else I have learned over time is that the world will not love our children like we do. Personally, I do my best to see the goodness in all. I believe there is goodness even amongst the most broken, and Lord knows there is a lot of brokenness in our world. Sometimes it takes longer to see the goodness hidden under the layers of hurt, pain, and struggle, but I believe goodness exists in all of us. Everyone desires to be loved and accepted. It's how God created us. I encourage you to be kind, gentle, understanding, encouraging, and forgiving. If you're in a relationship that has to part ways, figure out how to end it so all parties involved leave with a clear and understanding conscience.

As humans, I think we often compare ourselves to others, whether on how we look, what we wear, what we drive, how much money we make, what we've achieved, or who others perceive us to be. Social media has absolutely factored into how people perceive life and themselves in it. If you want to learn more on this, I encourage you to check out the book *Teen's Guide to Face-to-Face Connections in a Screen-to-Screen World.* This is an excellent book written by Jonathan McKee and his daughter, Alyssa McKee, and offers insight on real-life situations as well as tips to meaningful communication in a digital world. The *Social Dilemma*, a documentary on Netflix also offers insight.

While Benjamin was a huge gamer, he didn't spend a lot of time on social platforms playing the comparison game. He didn't need to. I think Ben compared himself to his siblings, cousins, and friends. While Benjamin was an average student, we were excited for him when he made the honor roll. However, his sisters' names typically appeared each quarter in the local newspaper, and they were also inducted into the National Honor Society. While Ben took a detour from college, Mandy and Carrie attended college and obtained their bachelor's degrees. As Ben stayed closer to home, he watched as both his sisters went abroad. Ben also witnessed his cousins and friends getting married and starting families while I imagine he was searching, waiting, and wondering who his person was or if she was even out there. I think Ben dreaded holidays and the persisting question that seemed to be the only topic of conversation for some: "Who are you dating?" or, "Are you dating anyone?" I think this inquiry reminded Ben of what wasn't happening in his life or where he thought others expected him to be, and that somehow may have given him the impression he had failed their expectations, which is so sad. I think we can all agree, nobody likes the feeling of failure or judgment. I think socials and gatherings such as this were just that and why Ben typically drove separately: to escape and make an early exit.

My wish for anyone who reads this book who may be struggling in a difficult relationship is for you to know you can recover. I've learned with God all things are possible. Pain may be overwhelming and all-encompassing. Removing yourself from this life because of whatever terrible situation you're in is not the resolve you seek. A driving force for suicide may be the thought that the person who has caused this excruciating pain will suffer with a broken heart when you die. Please let me reiterate, the people who will suffer from your absence and be left with feelings of anguish, shame, blame, pain, sadness, madness, despair, emptiness, brokenness, and devastation are the people who love you.

I know that I'm sharing my story, but I also know that each one of you reading this book has your own story as well. I'm confident your story, like all stories, includes the ebbs and flows that life brings. If you are one of those currently walking through a relentless storm, feeling hopeless and wanting to give up, please don't. Whether it's a broken relationship you desperately desire to fix, a difficult financial situation, a job you lost, a promotion you didn't get, the lover you wanted, the pregnancy you hoped for or the pregnancy you lost, or whatever "it" is, please know that it is possible to go on. There are people who are here to walk with you on your journey.

If you or someone you know is struggling or in crisis, call 911 or go to the nearest emergency room. Other resources include calling or texting 988, formerly known as the National Suicide Prevention Lifeline, or chat at 988lifeline.org. Trained counselors can help people experiencing a suicidal, substance use, and/or mental health crisis or any other emotional distress. People can also dial 988 if they are worried about a loved one who may need crisis support. You can also text HOME to 741741 from anywhere in the United States. This Crisis Line can handle any crisis. A live, trained counselor receives the text and responds, all from a secure online platform. The volunteer crisis counselor will help move you from a hot moment to a cool moment. These resources are available 24/7. Please utilize these services or check out afsp.org to find a support group near you. BENS Hope is just one of the many resources available.

Terry and I created BENS Hope to serve as a resource and ministry to help you move forward knowing you are not alone. Ben will forever be remembered as being kind and selfless. We honor him by offering kindness to others and being selfless in our pursuit of suicide awareness and prevention as well as our desire to offer the much-needed hope that people are seeking.

Please know that it is possible to get beyond whatever you're struggling with. I am not saying it will be easy, but I am saying it is possible. I pray you stay in this world so your loved ones never have to experience what life is like without you here.

※

Be joyful in hope, patient in affliction, faithful in prayer.
Romans 12:12 (NIV)

CHAPTER 3

INVASIVENESS AND QUESTIONING

*Do not let any unwholesome talk come out of your mouths, but only
what is helpful for building others up according to their needs,
that it may benefit those who listen.*
Ephesians 4:29 (NIV)

Ben left us November 11, 2014, and not a day goes by without him in my thoughts. Words cannot express the magnitude of how much I love and miss my son. I recall feeling overwhelmed and, through sobbing tears, had a conversation with God reciting how nobody understood the depths of my pain or how much I missed Ben. I reminded God, like He had forgotten, that it was I who carried Benjamin in my womb for nine months and birthed him into the world regardless of anyone who knew or loved him, and nobody could *ever* love him more than me, his mom. And then came God's loving response, "I do." I was speechless. Oh my goodness, of course our Heavenly Father understood! Because as much as I loved Ben, He loved him more! He loves all of us more than we can imagine. What tremendous love! Then I realized God loves us so much that He gave His only Son as a sacrifice because of His great love for me and you. I came to the conclusion that God blesses us with children, grandchildren, and pets to give us a glimpse of an idea of how much He loves us. I await the love in God's Kingdom because it is beyond anything that earth has to offer.

No, in all these things we are more than conquerors through Him who loved us. For I am sure that neither death nor life, nor angels nor rulers, nor things present nor things to come, nor powers, nor height nor depth, nor anything else in all creation, will be able to separate us from the love of God in Christ Jesus our Lord.
Romans 8:37-39 (ESV)

Nothing will ever replace Ben or the space in my heart that he filled. I miss hugging my son and seeing his smile, especially the "Ben Face" he was notably known for and the accusations it implied. Ben displayed this look at times when he was trying to be modest but was excited about something that he may or may not have elected to disclose to us. We still lovingly reference the Ben Face when opportunities present themselves within our family, stating, "Oh look, Mom (or whoever) has the Ben Face." Of course, this enduring term warms our hearts and reminds us of Ben. On holidays especially, I find myself looking at the front window, longing for Ben's car to pull up, speakers blaring, and then awaiting his entrance into the house to embrace and exchange a welcome home hug. I miss his bounding down the stairs as he returned from hanging with his friends. I also miss sneaking kisses on his forehead as he lie sleeping or just smelling him. If you're a parent, you understand this smelling thing, right? Who would have ever imagined the healthy, little boy I brought into the world, gave butterfly kisses to on his cheeks, snuggled, read bedtime stories to, and awaited glowing smiles from each morning from his crib would one day die by suicide. Definitely not me. All these years later, Ben's decision to take his life is still surreal. I remember asking God one day why me, why us?! His response: "Why not?" Believing in God or having faith does not mean you live a life free of hurt, loss, pain, or suffering. But because we know Him or may come to know Him in such circumstances of brokenness and desperation, it is possible to move forward and even experience joy again. It is a journey we continue walking on and working through every day.

Blest are those who mourn, for they shall be comforted.
Matthew 5:4 (NKJV)

Even though it's been years, there are days when it seems like yesterday and yet other times when it seems like my longing for Ben has been an eternity. For us, getting through each day is a triumph. I recall initially making it through minute by minute, one at a time. Then surviving minutes turned into surviving hours, days, and years. People reassured me I was strong and would get through this loss. I recall asking them, "Do you know how many seconds are in a minute and minutes in an hour and hours in a day?" Every second is another one without your loved one here and, instead, one of survival. For me, God's been my strength in the moments when I'm alone, sobbing uncontrollably from the depths of my soul, wondering how to go on, times too innumerable to share. In many instances, it's just me and my faith. I recall one day making it to work and my boss stopping by, asking what I had accomplished that day. My response was, "I got up, dressed, I'm here, and I'm breathing." And let me tell you, this was a huge feat for me! At that point, I was still trying to decide if I wanted to stay in this world. My prayer is if you haven't lost your child, please offer compassion for those who have and support them as they move forward on their grief and healing journey. It's important for those of us who have gone through a loss to have grace for others who haven't. We only know what we know.

I used to wake up every morning reciting the same phrase: I can't believe Ben is gone. After months of this vicious cycle, something came to me. I needed to address my reality and retrain my brain versus staying in the cycle of disbelief. So every morning I would tell myself that Ben was gone, he died by suicide, and this was my new reality.

After crying out multiple times to God, one morning specifically I recall reaching out in desperation, questioning how to go on without Ben here. God's response was, "Time here is but a sliver to all eternity." It's true. Our time here is limited, friends, but after death comes eternal life, and believers will be reunited with their loved ones. It brings me comfort knowing I will see my son again.

I truly believe if Ben could have known the pain his suicide would cause his family, he would not have taken his life, because he would never wish to hurt us. But he was apparently in a place so dark he was unable to think outside of his own circumstances. What these circumstances all entailed remain a mystery.

Since Ben's decision to end his life, we have reeled in our own struggles to heal. Books were sought to aid in processing a family tragedy of this magnitude. Some books were suggested, while others I came across on my own. Each story is as important and unique as the person writing and sharing it. I specifically recall after Ben's suicide being referred to read the book *No Time to Say Goodbye* by Carla Fine. We called the Platteville Public Library, asked for the four copies they had available, and started reading. The book offered guidance through various stages of the survival process. It definitely made suicide more real and validated the number of others who died by suicide and the impact on loved ones left behind. But questions remained.

I had no idea I would be writing a book, but four weeks after Ben's suicide, God instructed me to start journaling. Initially, I told God that I didn't have the capacity to journal, and how dare He ask! It took all I had to get through each hellish day. But God persisted, saying that His Son Jesus's death happened so people's lives could be saved and that this book would save lives and help others. God said the title of the book would be *Tears of Love*. And here it is!

Please note that the entries from my journal were written going back eight years. As I scanned through them, I knew I had to express my sincere gratitude to those mentioned, those who continue to support me on my journey, and those who were in my life and have moved on in theirs. I am not proclaiming to have things figured out, but sharing my personal journal entries depicting the time after my son Benjamin's suicide is important. I am hopeful that by sharing my story, this book may offer comfort and insight, whether you're a survivor of suicide, have a desire to learn more about suicide, are struggling yourself, or are supporting a loved one who is.

What I know from my personal experience is the loss of a loved one I classify as "my person" has caused me excruciating pain. But the pain that accompanies the loss of your child takes pain to a whole new level that cannot be put into words. It's a pain that can only be known if you've lived it because we only know what we know based on our life circumstances. I've learned this suffering seeps into every crevice and fiber of your being. This pain runs as deep as your love for them. If you haven't experienced the loss of your child or children, I pray you never do. If you have, my heart goes out to you. Hugs, my friend.

I want you to know that our family has experienced a number of painstaking losses, many with younger family members, which are addressed in a later chapter. But Ben's death was different. First for the obvious reason, Benjamin was my son, our child. But by suicide? The act and reality of suicide is a beast. Suicide has many layers to it. It's complex, invasive, and leaves you with countless questions, most which will never be answered. You're left trying to make sense out of something that will never make sense.

From conversations I've had with others survivors, I learned family members are typically blindsided by their loved one's suicide. We're left with such guilt that we were not able to save them and shame because our love was not enough. I share this insight, previously unknown to me.

PHASE 1: INVASIVENESS, CONFISCATION AND QUESTIONS

Being a survivor of suicide, I am better aware of the complexity and various facets that accompany it. In addition to being a horrific loss, Ben's suicide also involved an interrogation, an investigation, and a confiscation of personal belongings. This obviously amplified the agony of dealing with Ben's death. There is so much confusion. Did this really happen? Am I stuck in a nightmare? Is this my real life? Why would my loved one do this? Was it actually a homicide? Who is responsible for this? The reality of accepting that Ben—or for you, your loved one—took his life and holding him accountable is just so much to process or has been for me, personally.

Then there are the questions—countless, relentless questions. I recall being at one of our first SOS meetings hosted by Journey Mental Health in Madison, Wisconsin. A gentleman survivor spoke up saying that having millions of questions is typical, and from his personal experience in losing his brother to suicide, while answers may be found for some questions, others will never come, and eventually, we need to find peace in this. As time has gone by, how true we have found his statement to be. I thank God for the numbing He provides to shield us initially when such a tragedy occurs so we don't feel the full magnitude of pain. I'm not sure it would be possible to withstand or survive otherwise. Then I believe the numbing starts to thaw, and feelings become more prevalent as we work through the circumstances that have become our new reality. That must be why the same gentleman told us that if we thought the first year was difficult, wait until the second. I didn't appreciate his comment; it actually angered me profusely. I thought, *Buddy, you have no idea the amount of pain this mama's enduring,* but we would learn he was speaking from his experience, and we found this statement to be true as well.

Since starting our SOS support meetings, the most common questions are: Why did this happen? What did I/we/they do wrong? How could I/we/they have prevented this? How could I/we/they not see this coming? For those thinking a suicide is obvious to detect, let me reassure you that's not always the case.

Below are a series of emails between Ben and myself the day before his suicide.

From: Ben Cullen [mailto:ben.cullen@kaplan.com]
Sent: Monday, November 10, 2014 8:23 AM
To: Patti A. Cullen
Subject: winter tire purchase

Morning Mom, So I lucked out as we didn't have any snow on the ground this morning, had a bit of rain but still too warm for anything to stick yet, it's supposed to start getting colder tonight and all throughout the week so I think we're going to start seeing snow accumulate tonight and later this week. I talked with one of my coworkers this morning and he said Eau Claire already got 5 inches and more on the way, since we're closer to winter then I thought I'm going to use the money I have in my savings to buy some winter tires.

After talking with my coworker Tim, he told me about these Blazek snow tires which are supposed to do very well in snow. I did some searching and I think I found a pair that isn't too unreasonable for the price, especially for what they do. I wanted to wait a little closer to Black Friday to see if I could find a deal but these are only $75 each and if I can get them on before we get more snow I'd feel much safer about making my morning commute when the ground is still frozen over and ice may be around.

From: Patti A. Cullen
Sent: Monday, November 10, 2014 10:37 AM
To: Ben Cullen
Subject: RE: winter tire purchase

Hi Honey, I was going to text you and see if you'd gotten snow…glad you didn't yet; would definitely encourage you to get tires on sooner than later…Confident you'll feel better and safer too, Ben. Do you know someone that can put them on and get them balanced for you? Another option may be going to Farm and Fleet…close by and can happen today or tomorrow versus waiting on getting tires…your call of course.

Wow, the Packers game was a blow out! Bears need to get back on board … don't think they played the game they wanted either.

Having a productive day…so much to do and get caught up on … as matter of fact…tomorrow is Veteran's Day and contemplating coming into work…

Carrie and I got up this morning and went to toning class at UWP…would have been so easy to sleep in, so glad that we got up for it. Never regret those workouts! Right?!

Have a great day!
Love you more,
Mom

Later in the day I received the following emails from Benjamin. As a banker, it was not unusual for my kids to ask questions or have conversations as the ones below, or so I thought.

From: Ben Cullen [mailto:ben.cullen@kaplan.com]
Sent: Monday, November 10, 2014 10:55 AM
To: Patti A. Cullen
Subject: co-signer on previous loans

Mom can you do me a favor and look through your emails or any documentation you have regarding my previous loans? I'm just wondering if you are a co-signer on any outstanding loans that I currently have.

From: Patti A. Cullen
Sent: Monday, November 10, 2014 11:18 AM
To: Ben Cullen <ben.cullen@kaplan.com>
Subject: RE: co-signer on previous loans

Yes, was cosigner on your Mound City Bank loan (as was dad)…maybe on prior school loans, but can't recall honey and didn't keep emails…sorry…

From: Ben Cullen [mailto:ben.cullen@kaplan.com]
Sent: Monday, November 10, 2014 3:04 PM
To: Patti A. Cullen
Subject: Re: FYI – Thanksgiving

Is there anything you guys have planned before thanksgiving?

From: Ben Cullen [mailto:ben.cullen@kaplan.com]
Sent: Monday, November 10, 2014 3:28 PM
To: Patti A. Cullen
Subject: Re: FYI – Thanksgiving

Was just seeing if you had any events or activities planned between now and thanksgiving.

From: Patti A. Cullen
Sent: Monday, November 10, 2014 4:31 PM
To: Ben Cullen <ben.cullen@kaplan.com>
Subject: RE: FYI – Thanksgiving

We welcome our kids home anytime!!! Packers games every Sunday!!! Confident dad would enjoy spending time with you as well, if you come home. I actually have training this Saturday to become a HOSPICE Volunteer; next weekend is a Poker Run benefit in Benton to support friend and co-worker Sarah Olson's mom's cancer benefit. You are WELCOME to join us. I WOULD LOVE TO HAVE YOU HERE!

From: Patti A. Cullen
Sent: Tuesday, November 11, 2014 8:47 AM
To: Ben Cullen <ben.cullen@kaplan.com>
Subject: Hey

Hi Honey, Bank is closed today, but I came into work…going to get a bunch of things done ☺ Few others here as well.

Wanted to check in w/you and see how much snow you got…we had a sprinkle of it here…did you get your tires ordered? Best to, sooner than later…

Also, were you thinking of coming home before Thanksgiving? Welcome to any time ☺ Have a great day honey ☺

Love you more ☺ Mom

There was no reply from Ben. I would never receive another email, text, or call from my son, ever.

The misery of failing your child is a horrendous place to be. I wasn't sure how to go on. My journal entries depict the pain and reality of Ben's suicide, the atrocious mountain climb ahead, and yet the hope that still trickled in.

These entries are categorized by subject over the next chapters versus chronologically, as initially written. God instructed me to journal following Ben's suicide because I would not be able to recall these raw feelings later. Please accept any apologies in advance for any content that is unsettling to readers mentioned in my journaling with consideration of dates entries were written.

12/12/2014

Who would have known that just four weeks ago today, our lives would change forever. Ben, our wonderful son/brother/grandson/nephew/ cousin/friend took his life by suicide. One path to healing, I know, is to write his story and express the raw and intense grief that comes with this reality. As the saying goes, this is a parent's worst nightmare. As Ben's mom, my worst nightmare became my new reality.

The night we learned of Ben's suicide will be forever engrained in our minds.

I hadn't heard from Ben all day. I usually have some form of communication with all my kids every day. Ben wasn't picking up his phone or returning texts, and it wasn't like him. Terry and I were watching TV that evening, and I had decided to call Caleb, Ben's roommate, to see if he had any news on Ben. When Caleb answered, nothing seemed out of the ordinary. He could hear music in Ben's room and figured he must be in there, gaming or something. We were on the phone with Caleb as he knocked then entered Ben's room. It only took a few short moments for us to overhear Caleb discover Ben unresponsive. Shock is an understatement. I'll always remember the frantic voice of Caleb repeating the words, NO, NO, NO, NO, NO, THIS IS NOT HAPPENING. As I listened on the other end of the phone, I was in disbelief, trying to make sense of Caleb's reaction to what he was witnessing and to what my mind was attempting to process. I literally felt the life in my body drain from my head to my toes as I went from sitting to standing. My breath exited my body, and I struggled to breathe as I continued trying to make sense of what had happened, but my mind was in shock, I couldn't process what was happening. Terry was instructing Caleb to call 911 and ensuring him that we would head to them immediately! This trip to get to our deceased son was the longest two-and-a-half-hour drive of our lives.

12/14/2014

As I stand by the kitchen sink and look outside, I think of Ben ... again. He's always on my mind. The extent of grief and sadness I've felt cannot be described, and the pain reaches into my soul. Will I ever be able to accept Ben's decision of suicide? If it's what he wanted, why am I in such despair? Feelings of emptiness and guilt constantly overwhelm me.

12/15/2014

Even with Ben's whispers always in my head, we must still, somehow, take care of ourselves. Get into a routine and back into life. One step at a time is enough. Today I got up, took the book I was reading to the treadmill, and walked for 45 minutes. It was a feeling of accomplishment, something I haven't felt lately.

Afterward, I spoke with my friend, Sue, on the phone for forty-five minutes and mentioned a recent incident that seemed to foreshadow Ben's death. At a bridal shower attended by a psychic medium, I was told to expect a "big event" around Thanksgiving that would bring our family closer together. Looking back now, I realize that Ben's life was predestined since birth, and there was nothing we could have done in those final weeks to change the outcome. Sue shared some of her own recent struggles and reminded me that we need to rely on God to see us through them. And once we're over the hurdles, we can feel a sense of growth and accomplishment. Our souls have grown stronger. I understood that Ben's death is also a lesson that will grow our souls and guide us to find goodness from this tragedy.

Terry and I needed a change of scenery and took a road trip to do some shopping. We had time to discuss how we could heal our grief-

stricken hearts. Tears overcame me on the trip home, and Terry put his arm around me in hopes of comforting me, even though he's mourning too. We're looking forward to helping others in this situation someday, honoring Ben's generous soul. As much as we miss him, we also feel honored to have had him as our son for 27 years. The love we shared is something some never experience and a blessing we will cherish forever.

12/16/2014

Woke up at 5:45 a.m.; Terry was already up for a couple hours. I tried going back to sleep but could only think of Ben, so I decided to get up too. I came across pictures on my computer from three years ago when I was struggling with where Terry and I were in our marriage. It reminded me of how desperate feelings can come when you feel your world is falling apart around you. It saddens my heart to think that Ben felt so alone and desperate. Even though he gave so much love, his heart was broken. The reality of Ben's suicide remains unfathomable. We still don't know how to accept it.

8:00 a.m.

We completed the thank you letters to Ben's workplace and returned a crockpot to our friend, Jenni, who'd sent us potato soup last week. I came across Ben's obituary and completely lost it. WHY, WHY, WHY?????? How could this happen?! How could Ben do this to us?!!! Tears of sadness overcame me...again. The grief, agony, sadness, despair, and mourning are beyond what I thought a person could bear. Sometimes I actually don't even recognize my own cries as I wail in a voice I don't recognize. Often, I weep alone because I feel others may be overwhelmed or distance themselves because of the fear they feel from the depth of my sadness. To me, my tears are now a symbol of the love I have for my son. But I know that these tears I cry only reflect the enormous amount of love that I have for my children. Now that Ben is no longer in my physical presence, my tears have become a symbol of the love I have for the son who meant the world to me...my Beno...

6:15 p.m.

Imagine yourself waiting for a hot air balloon to lift off. As you wait, you sit idle. Our sadness is in that place—on the ground, empty, anticipating something more. As time passes, we are hopeful the sadness will one day lift like a hot air balloon, rising as it brings the joys of feeling weightlessness and happiness. Feelings of peacefulness, calmness, and fulfillment where our hearts again feel joy and see all the beauty around us. A time when we can again enjoy all life has to offer.

12/17/2014

Woke up after 5:00 a.m. with the same realization as the days before. Benjamin is dead. As always, the day begins with so many questions and so few answers. We would have done ANYTHING to save/help/rescue Ben from whatever sadness and despair he was feeling. What I do know is that each time I envision Ben, he is smiling. I must find comfort knowing that the decision he made was his and that he has found the peace he desired.

12/19/2014

Fantastic visit with our good friends Sue, Shane, Eden, and Sophie who brought us our favorite pizza from Uno's. Of course, every visit encompasses discussion, tears, and memories of Ben. Sometimes for a moment, things feel normal. Then in the next second, our new reality returns. Ben's death is as real as heaven is to me. I long to talk to people who attempted to complete suicide but survived. I am trying to get an idea of what their thought process was. I compared the first couple of weeks after Ben's suicide of how I was feeling to what Ben may have felt like. Like Ben, I am surrounded by so many people who love and are willing to do anything for me, but I still feel alone, sad, and empty. When I think of Ben feeling like this, it saddens me profoundly. Was this Ben's reality? How horrible to think that externally he displayed such kindness while hiding his despair in a battle known only to himself.

12/21/2014

My daughter wasn't sure how to respond to her friend Melody's texts, which included Melody sharing that she was "officially dating." How do you respond to that? We wish Melody all the best. She is a beautiful, kind, and successful young lady with a big heart. But now I find myself questioning the reasoning why she suddenly had time to date after expressing to Ben that she didn't. While I have absolutely no intention of holding Melody responsible for Ben's suicide, I do know that Ben had fallen hard, as he typically did in each relationship. He gave one hundred percent and nothing less. Besides, it was Melody who had sought out Ben earlier this year. After initially declining to meet, he elected to hang out with Melody, after Carrie and my encouragement. It was wonderful to hear about their shared excursions. Ben's admiration for Melody was apparent from the get-go, and she shared with Carrie her appreciation for being treated so kindly by Ben.

Week of 1/5/2015

Terry attempted to return to work. He made it until 11:30 a.m. Monday and went in at 3:00 a.m. to plow snow Tuesday, but he ended up coming home early. I went to Harmony House every day for two to three hours for energy healing with Bonnie. Monday I had to drive to the bank drive-up to get cash. Big steps taken! Lots of looks from others, but I put on a brave face and marched forward, knowing Ben was with me and will be in my heart forever, helping as we all go forward on this journey. Tuesday was the eight-week marker. I cried that morning (again, a usual morning experience for me), missing Ben tremendously. Carrie went to school/work but was home within the hour, sobbing. Terry followed shortly after. It was a rough day for all of us reliving and questioning. What was Ben thinking eight weeks ago? We are all wondering why he just didn't reach out to us. We would have been there in an instant for him.

It seems that these questions are irrelevant at this point, as nothing will change the outcome. But for some reason, we still go back and look at everything. I guess it's because while we may never make sense of this, we still try to. If we can't help our loved ones, and in my case Benjamin, then I pray that at some point I will have an opportunity to share this story and save the lives of others. The warning signs were not as obvious as people may think. There was no history of depression, there were no doctor visits until recently, and even then, Ben's depression or thoughts of suicide were not apparent. My beautiful son is dead, and I cannot imagine what life will be like without him.

1/7/2015

Third day this week to get up and hop on the treadmill, even if only for 30 minutes. It's better to do something than do nothing. Showered afterward and then went off to my appointment at Harmony House. Spent the first forty-five minutes, as usual, talking; it's great therapy. Bonnie is a great listener, cares tremendously, and is a wonderful support system in addition to being a gifted healer. Enjoyed reflexology and Reiki after and was astonished by the sense of peace and calmness that encompassed me.

Today is Cullen Christmas, a tradition with Terry's extended family. Awake much during the night, constantly thinking about Ben and missing him tremendously. There are so many questions that we will never have answers to; we pray for his happiness and peace, and we will continue to find ours.

1/14/2015

Walked the treadmill again while reading; I also said my daily prayers. Mandy called in the morning and was quite upset about Ben. We talked for fifteen minutes or so while she expressed her concerns, trying to understand the reasoning for Ben's decision. We can all speculate and possibly rule out things, but not certain we will ever have all the answers to the questions we have. Terry made it through his third day at work. I returned to Harmony House for additional energy healing.

1/16/2015

As I find moments of solitude, there remains the underlying realization that my beautiful son, the love of my life, has exited this lifetime as a *physical being. While I remind myself that his spirit lives on, I find myself in deep sorrow, wishing I would have done something earlier that would have saved him from taking his life. I recall the conversation we had prior to him taking his life. He'd expressed concerns for feelings he was having. Ben also questioned the wisdom of seeking counseling at $400 a session, which seemed enormous. What neither of us considered was that it could be a matter of life and death for him. We hadn't discussed his insurance coverage or known about it at that time. Regardless, as in many conversations, I would explain to Ben that if money could resolve the issue, then it wasn't really a problem. We also talked about him taking medications. I expressed concerns to Ben about being aware that taking meds can have side effects and some as severe as suicidal thoughts ... never knowing that Ben was at such a point of despair that he would even consider it an option. Based on the medical reports we received recently, the records suggest Ben was not suicidal. Carrie asked if this information brought comfort to me, knowing that not even a medical professional could have diagnosed Ben, so how would I as his mom be able to?*

1/18/2015

Wow, what a beautiful sunny day. Got up and said my prayers knowing that today is a must for taking a walk outside. Carrie was up shortly after Terry and I got up. She had enjoyed a day with her boyfriend, Matt, in Dubuque on Saturday and a belated Christmas celebration with her volleyball team. She caught up with the girls and shared how many of them were engaged, married, and/or had children. Carrie then told us she was struggling. At first, I thought she meant she struggled with the concept that others were married or with child. But she was struggling with Ben's death and with the reality that others cannot relate to such a tragedy. She was struggling with how she was supposed to deal with the tremendous amount of grief and how you move on from it. I shared that the grief we felt might've been only a fraction of grief that Benjamin felt. I told Carrie that I have felt such extreme sadness on multiple occasions since Ben's death, with the belief that these feelings came forth so I can have some appreciation for the depth of sadness that Ben must have felt.

This didn't seem to be of comfort to Carrie. She said, "Yes, but he killed himself so he didn't have to deal with the pain." She questioned what was left for us to do. She wondered if we are just left here to suffer from his actions and deal with the pain he elected to rid of himself. She said it didn't seem fair or make sense, but that none of this does at this point. My heart broke knowing that she was feeling such despair. We desperately want happiness for our children. Living with our new reality and knowing of Ben's sadness is more than I can bear. But here I find myself again, dealing with Carrie's sadness, aware that while I am here to love and comfort her, the healing that must occur is actually something Carrie will need to grieve through in order to heal. It sucks. And there is no other way at this moment to actually describe it.

Adapting to this new reality that Ben is no longer physically here is not something that I can just get over. It has been ten weeks today, which means that ten weeks and one day ago, Ben was still here and every day before that for twenty-seven years. Happiness had been something I felt every day. Now I pray for the days when I'll feel true happiness again. I also pray that I don't let my sadness sink me. I know with all my heart that I desire to bring comfort, love, and hope to others because of our tragedy. With that in mind, it gives me strength to believe that good will come from this and that helping others will help our family feel whole again.

As for now, I'm just taking one day at a time. I find it hard to believe that it's 2015. I've lost track of time and only know that my mission is to get through life day by day. I continue to wake up each morning and say hello to Ben, Dad, Greg, Abby, and other loved ones in spirit. I pray daily for others and for us. I pray that goodness may come and that one day we will understand God's grand plan.

But at this point, it's not making sense. I have faith that there will be brighter days ahead with God's love. He is carrying our family during this time. I pray for Ben to forgive me for not encouraging him to seek counseling or take meds. I pray he forgives us for not being better attuned to the depth of his sadness or for not seeing that he feared appearing weak if he shared his inner feelings. I question if I should have pushed harder when I attempted to have a conversation with him about his friend Melody and why their relationship/friendship ceased instead of avoiding it after Ben made it clear this topic was not up for discussion.

Unfortunately, this is a lesson that we must all learn as we go forward. I pray for the day that my spiritual relationship with Ben will grow, and I will find comfort in a new relationship with him. I also pray for the day that I will actually see him again.

1/25/2015

Terry and I returned from our getaway in Dubuque on Sunday evening. Decided on our way home that I really wanted to listen to the greeting from Ben's cell phone that UScellular had emailed me, so I did. I crumbled apart when I got home, and I wept for his presence. I don't wish to burden Ben with my sadness, so I apologize when I cry, but again, there are so many tears of love to be shed that are just in proportion to the depth of love I have for my Beno. That night I couldn't fall asleep. Still so many questions, so few answers, such guilt, sadness, memories, and love for Ben. God help us all to find comfort and peace. God help us find the goodness that will come from this.

1/30/2015

I'm not sure why this is an extra yucky morning, but it is. Lots of tears and missing Ben. So many questions and apologies for Ben. Where did we go wrong? How did I mess him up so badly? Did I love him too much, and the world was too mean? What should we have done differently? I'm mad, sad, pissed, angry, and know that regardless of what I say or do, nothing will bring Ben back into his physical body to be with us again.

Recovery from losing Ben this way is going to take an unknown amount of time. I yelled at Ben earlier. I know he didn't think this far ahead. We were available to help him when he was alive, but he didn't want to burden us. Now his death is a heavy weight we carry each day. We're trying to muddle through and figure out how the hell to do this. This surely isn't getting any easier. I imagine if he'd known what would be left behind, he wouldn't have even considered suicide. Then again, Ben *obviously wasn't in the frame of mind that we thought. And for that, I'm truly sorry.*

Feeling that I failed as his mom is putting it lightly. Ben was a wonderful, beautiful, kind, considerate, loving, giving son, and I remind myself that I would rather have had the relationship and experience with him for twenty-seven years than not to have had him at all. He was truly a gift and blessing in my life, and for that I will forever be grateful. I just miss him so terribly. There are moments when I don't know how life can go on. I am giving it to God and asking for His guidance. Only He can see the grander picture that is just a blur to me.

2/5/2015

Terry invited me to join him to meet Rick, a counselor at UW-Platteville. We shared our stories, and Rick paid his deepest condolences to us. He also shared a lot of information about ADD, a condition Ben was diagnosed with in elementary school. I expressed my frustration at having agreed to put Benjamin into learning development (LD) classes and felt that the experience was humiliating to Ben. Rick reassured us that ADD does not automatically imply a student is in need of LD classes, but unfortunately, that's what happens. He said students with ADD are typically very intelligent, which we knew Benjamin was. But he also said depression is a component of ADD, something we didn't recall hearing before. I felt very sad that there was such a lack of information from the school about understanding Ben's condition. Going forward, this information will be useful to help others. A two-hour energy healing was calming and comforting, and that evening Terry and I enjoyed Chinese and stayed in to watch American Idol auditions. We went to bed at 10:30 p.m., and I realized that in the past four hours, while we watched TV, 12 people had died by suicide. It will be a gift from God to educate others on depression and suicide so lives can be saved.

2/13/2015

I've been dreading my birthday this year. There will be no text from Ben extending birthday wishes, which is something I've always cherished from my boy. I woke up and spent hours thinking of Ben, missing him, and asking questions I've repeatedly asked without getting answers. I don't want to keep feeling guilty about what should have or could have been done. More than that it is the void of a love that will never be replaced. Knowing I must live with this new reality is just more than I can imagine some days. Today, my birthday, is one of them. What I have noticed lately is the appreciation I have for Terry. He has quite the shoes to fill for me and the girls as a hubby, dad, friend, and advisor. He's become so compassionate; I know he'll give all he can to us.

Terry brought me breakfast in bed, which was so sweet; he gave me toasted cinnamon bread and an orange. We stayed in bed a while longer, which was a very nice feeling, being so close to him. He also special-ordered a birthday cake with strawberry filling, my favorite! He also presented a beautiful card and a bag of M&Ms plus a gift card to Harmony House from him and the girls. Terry also bought a rose and baby's breath. The attached card read, "I know Ben couldn't get you something, so I wanted to." I prayed and asked Ben to show me signs today that would bring comfort and reassurance that he is still with me/us.

My friend, Meghan, stopped by with a gift and card. She worked for the county at the time and attended my sister-in-law Jenny's church. Meghan had attempted suicide in high school and had put prayer out that she could help others who were struggling, and her prayer and ours were answered when we met her. She shared that if she had been born a boy, her parents would have named her Benjamin. That offered comfort and was a Godwink that God had brought us together. The gift was a metal-edged ornament of a mother holding her son. The card read, "Faith is being sure of what we hope for and certain of what we do not see." Hebrews 11:1. Inside she wrote, "Happy Birthday to one of the most caring, giving, and faith-filled women I have ever met. I am beyond thankful God made our paths cross. He has amazing things in store for you!! I am honored to be able to honor Benjamin's life through God's plan in our upcoming journey of offering hope to those hurting. I feel as though I've known you for years. I love that about our relationship. Enjoy yourself today (and every day), you deserve it."

Needless to say, I took Meghan's surprise visit as a sign from Ben, one that made me smile through my tears. We also got to meet Byron, her one-year-old son who is precious. It was love at first sight. After Meghan left, Terry and I headed to the cemetery to place a rose at Ben's gravesite. As expected, the visit was excruciating. As I lay the rose upon Ben's grave, the reality of Ben's death swept through me again. I walked back through the snow to the car and wept uncontrollably. Terry extended his hand to comfort me. There was no comforting me in my sadness, madness, despair, anger, confusion, and frustration. This situation is not fair. Ben should not be dead. What did we do to deserve this suffering?

How could our son, who had such a giving and loving soul, break? Why did he fall victim to his despair while so many careless idiots continue roaming the universe? Somehow, I must make sense of this. I must find the goodness in it. I must not fall victim to this. I must focus on what good can come from it and how the tragedy we've endured can bring hope to others.

As Terry and I left the cemetery, my cell phone fell from my purse I was holding on my lap. As I picked up my phone, I noticed the time. 11:11. The date of Ben's death. A date that will forever be ingrained in my brain. It was a sign to me that Ben is still with us. It was bittersweet. I'd asked for signs and felt Ben was giving them to me. I had to appreciate his efforts and become more familiar with our new spiritual relationship—the relationship that will remind me we will always be together with our departed loved ones in a new way.

2/16/2015

Awake a lot during the night, stressing out about how to go back to work. Missing Benjamin beyond words. Tears continue to flow. I realize that others have moved forward or gone back to their lives while we try to figure out how we go on. It is unbelievably difficult thinking about going forward without Ben. Sometimes I think of how many more years I will be on this earth before I will be with Ben again. I look forward to seeing him. I also find myself feeling badly about these thoughts and know that I need to focus on life each day. Find the blessings and the fact that I have a wonderful loving family around to support us and celebrate life ahead.

I need to keep faith in God that we will get through this. But as I say my morning prayers, I find myself weeping again. My heart is broken, and I can't make sense of how loving someone as much as I loved Ben could end in a death. Why did his heart feel empty? Where did we go wrong? What didn't we do right? I continue asking the same questions, over and over like a broken record, but never find resolve. It's a vicious cycle, and I feel at times I'm part of the movie Groundhog Day, a movie I despised and now feel I'm living in.

I went to see a medium to discuss the best way to get a list of people we could invite to attend SOS. She invited me into her office afterward. We visited a while, and before long, she was receiving messages from Ben. She said she knows how much I love my family and each of our kids. And while she knows I love our girls profusely, she noticed that there was some difference with my relationship with Ben. I shared that Ben was our first child, our only son, but she asked for more. I shared that when I was pregnant with Ben, Terry and I had some challenges. Terry was overwhelmed at becoming a new father and taking on the responsibilities of the home we'd recently purchased.

I stated that at one point, I felt such despair that I contemplated going into the garage, sitting in the car, and letting it run. But then I felt Ben kicking in my tummy, which brought me back to reality. I questioned what I was thinking. She elaborated that I felt Ben had saved me at that moment, and in turn, I now carried guilt that I should have saved him. There was truth to this! I hadn't considered this consciously, but when she spoke those words, it brought me to tears. She later shared that Ben was sending reassurance of the happiness he had felt when he was with his family. While women typically are more empathetic than men, Ben, being an empath himself, carried the weight of a lot of emotions and feelings. He wasn't always sure what to do with these feelings.

The sadness he carried was not from his family but from a sense of loss for the sadness he felt others endured. She also shared that his relationships with Melody and his boss, Jaren, definitely factored into his recent struggles, but neither are responsible for his final actions.

During our session, she explained that Ben apologized for having sent Melody the text before taking his life. He said that was selfish of him, and he doesn't want me to go through life carrying this weight or guilt. He did what he felt at the time and was sorry for being selfish. He felt overwhelmed in life knowing that Melody and Carrie were friends, and even if he and Melody went their separate ways, he would have to encounter Melody with Carrie. At the time, this was too much for him to bear. Ben was reassuring us of the love he shared with his family. Her insight was helpful with validation that Benjamin is still around all of us.

After the session with her, I went to Harmony House to see Bonnie. The medium had asked that I have Bonnie do energy work on healing my emotional sadness and remorse for not having saved Benjamin. While we gave this intention, I was so absolutely exhausted from the energy it had taken to get this far. I basically passed out in the chair while Bonnie performed reflexology and Reiki. I slept so deeply that it was a challenge to wake myself up and walk out to my car to drive home. But what a sense of peace and comfort my time at the Harmony House brought.

2/18/2015

I had a restless night and didn't sleep well at all. I woke up early and helped Carrie make monkey bread for her supervisor's birthday. I went to work and tried my best to read emails. The ones that I read just didn't make sense, and I couldn't process them. I was overwhelmed once again. I spent time in Kari's office with her and Barb talking about my situation and feelings. They are great listeners and supporters. I am so grateful for them. I left work at 11:30 a.m. and headed home. Terry and I made pizza for lunch and met with two gals from UW-Platteville, Kayla and Jessica. These young ladies had asked us if we would be interested in a collaborative effort to host a 5K walk/run to promote mental health and suicide awareness. *After conversing with them for an hour, their offer sounded appealing. We have a few more things to figure out, but as of now, it sounds like this is a go! Went with Terry to city hall afterward to check out the room for our SOS meetings. It is not exactly what I was hoping for, but it will suffice and is a neutral location for all involved. Appointment with Bonnie at Harmony House at 2:00 p.m. was so needed. I actually passed out while she was talking, I was so exhausted. Had a huge snowfall that covered the earth with snowflakes...so pretty. But I'm actually ready for spring. I worked on our checkbook in the afternoon and spent time journaling also. Feeling like my writing is becoming a book and may benefit others in the future.*

2/23/2015

I worked half a day at the bank. While I've had a tremendous outpouring of love and support, the stress from my immediate boss is too much to bear. I now understood why I had diarrhea last night and again this morning. For now, I must go through the emotions of continuing my work here. I can't begin to explain the amount of courage and energy it takes to continue to work at the bank. I only know that by the time I leave each afternoon, I am completely exhausted. While others may question the limited hours of my return, I commend myself for conquering each hour I'm there. None of my coworkers have lost a child and can't relate to my position. I must stay true to what I feel I need to do and not worry about what others think or feel. What I do know, God forbid, is that if this should happen to any of them, others will look to me for support on how to grieve from the loss of a child, especially a suicide. For their sake, I pray this never happens to any of them.

I went to the Harmony House following work. I love Bonnie. No wonder her last name is Doll. She is just that...and a sweetheart. I'm always welcomed with a smile and open arms. She is a wonderful person with a beautiful soul. I can feel the comfort that I experience with the Reiki and reflexology she has been providing to me these past weeks. My demeanor is always in a much better place when leaving than when I arrive. Carrie invited Terry and me to watch her play volleyball tonight at the armory.

3/5/2015

Today is Ben's birthday; I woke at 3:25 a.m. Twenty-eight years ago, I would have been awake after giving birth to Benjamin at 2:55 a.m. The early wake-up call was fitting. I recalled what a blessing it was to hold our beautiful son in my arms. He was so tiny with lots of wrinkled skin, but it was love at first sight. I later remembered that after Ben's birth I noticed that the doctor and nurses in the room weren't saying anything, nor was my baby crying. He appeared blue in color, and I asked them if our baby was dead. But seconds later, I heard the beautiful cry of our son. He was perfect, and he was ours, a beautiful gift from God. I realized how blessed I was that our baby was OK. I whispered, "Happy Birthday," to Ben, now in spirit and in the loving arms of Jesus. He is happy now, and that was what I always wanted for him.

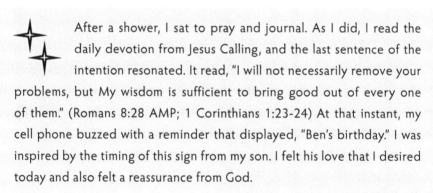 After a shower, I sat to pray and journal. As I did, I read the daily devotion from Jesus Calling, and the last sentence of the intention resonated. It read, "I will not necessarily remove your problems, but My wisdom is sufficient to bring good out of every one of them." (Romans 8:28 AMP; 1 Corinthians 1:23-24) At that instant, my cell phone buzzed with a reminder that displayed, "Ben's birthday." I was inspired by the timing of this sign from my son. I felt his love that I desired today and also felt a reassurance from God.

Mom arrived a few minutes before 8:00 a.m. Pam joined us, and the three of us were off for a memorable day to the Lions Eye Bank of Wisconsin in Madison. While my immediate family declined my invite for this visit, I felt strongly about going today on Ben's birthday. It was a tribute to him. After learning Ben's corneas had been donated to recipients in Wisconsin, I yearned to learn more about something he had contributed to. I figured our visit at 10:00 a.m. would be brief. Imagine our surprise when we left the facility at 12:30 p.m.! What an extraordinary group of people. They were so appreciative to meet us as Ben's donor family. In turn, we were overwhelmed to experience their deepest compassion for our loss and genuine appreciation for Ben's gifted donation. A new gal who came on

board a day before also had prior experience in tissue retrieval and knew the ins and outs of the process from beginning to end. They listened to our many questions and comforted us with the answers they provided. Our time there reinforced our appreciation of the respect, kindness, and consideration they'd shown us. It was obvious their involvement goes beyond being just a job. These positions involve much more that comes from the heart.

I would like to take this opportunity to share how Ben's corneas and tissue donations have blessed others.

LIONS EYE BANK

Two people were blessed with Ben's donation of his two corneas.

VERSITI DONATIONS

In addition, the donation of Ben's tissue has resulted in the preparation of 194 tissue implants, which have been or will be used in medical procedures to help others. A note dated February 22, 2019, from Versiti Organ and Tissue states that reporting of tissue recipient information by hospitals and surgeons is voluntary, and the degree of detail provided varies. Here's how Ben's gift of donated tissues can help recipients.

Donations of Ben's bone tissues can be used in spinal surgeries, dental procedures, and reconstructive surgeries to repair broken bones.Donations of Ben's connective tissue can be used to repair injuries involving the knee, ankle, and shoulder.

Donations of Ben's skin tissues can be used in urology surgeries, hernia repairs, wound coverings, post-mastectomy breast reconstruction, and coverings for burn victims. Skin can also be used by plastic surgeons to repair defects in the breasts, lips, and face.

Donations of Ben's vascular tissue can be used to restore circulation for people with diseased or damaged veins in their legs.

Donations of Ben's pericardium tissue (the thin covering around the heart) can be used as a protective covering over the brain after brain surgery and can be used during eye surgery.

Based upon information received, at least 122 individual lives have been transformed through Ben's gift of tissue donation. Ben's gift of donated tissue was used in procedures for male and female recipients ranging from seventeen to ninety-one years old throughout the country, including in Massachusetts, Indiana, South Carolina, Connecticut, Kansas, California, and Idaho. Funeral Director Matt Melby acknowledged us for being very generous with Ben's donations We reminded Matt, this decision was Ben's doing.

3/6/2015

Friday. Interestingly enough, I started dreading this day a few days ago. Terry felt compelled to make the trip to La Crosse to join some of Ben's colleagues for lunch. This invite came during Ben's funeral luncheon from Wendy and Asha, Ben's supervisor and colleague. Both women were such beautiful and wonderful people. While I appreciated the offer, I absolutely dreaded the thought of making this trip, the same route we'd driven the night of Ben's suicide.

The thought of it was much too painful; reliving the agony of that night was more than I could bear. While Terry and I had agreed to the visit, I was now questioning our decision. As the date grew closer, my anxiety had increased tremendously. How could this be a good idea? I felt Ben's guidance had encouraged me to ask someone outside of Terry and me to be present as a distraction for this ride down memory lane. I am grateful my nephew, Derek, was able to go with us. I was overwhelmed by tears all morning, and we hadn't even left the house. I questioned how the day would go. As I exited the bathroom, Terry greeted me with a hug, which I accepted, and I moved onward to Derek, who quietly awaited me in the living room. As I embraced him, I stood, hugging and sobbing. His presence was such a powerful reminder of Benjamin. He represents so much of Ben. I composed myself, and we headed out, ironically in Ben's car. Our car acted up on our last trip, so we figured Ben's car was our best bet for the trip to La Crosse. I shared landmarks along the way and places we'd stop on our travels to visit Ben and Mandy on our trips to La Crosse. Fennimore for cheese curds was a must and The Cakery & Bake Shop in Viroqua was also! Valley Market in Coon Valley was another usual stop before we'd drive into La Crosse and get to Ben's...this is where the most tears came.

As we drove to the restaurant to meet the Kaplan folks, we realized the building sat parallel to the Kaplan building where Ben had taken us to a few times. He was so proud of his accomplishments there, and we were too. We had Ben's parking permit, but there were no spots on the ramp. I prayed aloud, asking for Ben to help us find a front parking spot so we could do this. As we drove back down, still seeking parking, we got to the bottom floor, and what did we find...a front-row parking spot! Thank you, Beno...he was listening. Wendy, Asha, Caleb, and Tiffany were our guests for lunch. After exchanging hugs and tears, we reminisced for the next two hours. It was comforting being in the company of those who missed Benjamin like we did. The sadness they still felt was apparent and confirmed we are not alone in mourning the loss of someone amazing.

The Lord is near the brokenhearted and saves the crushed in spirit.
Psalm 34:18 (ESV)

CHAPTER 4

INTERROGATIONS AND JUDGEMENTS

Do not judge or you too will be judged. For in the same way you judge
others, you will be judged, and with the measure you use, it will be
measured to you. Why do you look at the speck of sawdust in your
brother's eye and pay no attention to the plank in your own eye?
Matthew 7:1 (NIV)

Ben's suicide involved an interrogation by the officials. We get it,
it's protocol. But outside of the officials asking questions, there
were others with interrogation mindsets and judgments galore. When
you're at the lowest of lows trying to cope with the loss of your loved
one to suicide, what isn't helpful is this judgment from others. Maybe
some of you understand this. Maybe others of you are judging. From
my personal perspective, there is one who will judge all of us, and it
isn't anyone holding this book.

PHASE 2: INTERROGATIONS AND JUDGMENTS

Experiencing loss, you typically feel the love and support of others
at the onset of the loss and in the days that follow. However, when the
loss is due to a suicide, there is a stigma that accompanies the initial
support. It was unlike any other loss I've experienced before. I realize

some of the judgments I put upon myself, while further judgments were accentuated by others. This caused deep pain, amplifying a horrific loss. My request is, please don't judge survivors; we do plenty of that ourselves. For the inquiring minds and those making judgments, let me assure you that nobody desires to fill in the blanks and have their questions answered more than the survivors. We understand your curiosity but ask for your empathy.

I will share that to avoid such judgment, our family found solace at the Millennium Cinema in Platteville. Our getaways to this safe haven were easily accessible. We could access our car from our garage that is attached to our house. We attended numerous matinees during the weekdays and encountered few, if any, others in the dark theater. These experiences offered a change of scenery, a somewhat sense of normalcy, and fulfilled our desire to get out of the house. So thankful for the Millennium Cinema.

Following are journal entries addressing both internal and external scenarios of judgements, whether intentional or not, and in some cases, from both sides. Some events may resonate with survivors while others may not.

12/21/2014

Sunday was a lazy day for the most part. Stayed in PJs, enjoyed snacking and watching football. As tired as we were, Terry and I didn't take any naps. Carrie watched a football game with her boyfriend, Matt, then came home early that evening. Carrie was getting text messages from Melody, her friend, who happened to be a young woman Ben had been seeing.

Ben's admiration for Melody was apparent from the get-go, and she shared with Carrie her appreciation for being treated as kindly by Ben as she'd desired from a guy, unlike her previous boyfriend. Melody had a giving spirit, much like Ben. Maybe that's what attracted him to her. Even though Ben and Melody were never "official," the experiences they shared and their time spent together meant the world to Ben. He enjoyed their time together profusely. After Ben's death, I recall the first meeting

I encountered with a psychic medium. She specifically asked if Ben had depression and if there was a girl that factored into Ben's sadness. While I've elected to not be a judge in this, what I do believe is Ben's sadness was related to being without a companion. His sadness and depression may have contributed to his suicide.

12/22/2014

We needed to do errands, but I wasn't prepared for my mixed emotions when I went outside and found Ben's car running with Terry behind the wheel. Again, I was swept away by tears and the memories that came. Was Ben there to reassure me he was OK? At the store, I ran into a woman I recognized from town. She came over and asked if she could give me a hug. "Of course," I answered. Love and hugs from others gave us the strength to help get through this. We reflected on Ben and the kind person he was, and I assured her our family would make sure goodness came from this tragedy. I thanked her for acknowledging us, knowing very well that she could have easily walked by us as most, or at least many, people do. Later in our trip to the store, my eyes met those of a woman who'd recently lost her child in an accident. We exchanged hellos as she walked by. But we both turned back, and she reached out to me. I wept softly as she embraced me. I could sense her sincerity. We extended words and shared thoughts before parting ways and wishing each other a Merry Christmas. As I walked out of the store, I wondered what others thought as they looked our way, knowing of Ben's death. Maybe it was their intent to avoid us at all costs. They were fortunate to have dodged this type of bullet. It shouldn't matter what others think, but it does cross your mind.

12/23/2014

Woke up after midnight, sensing something. I couldn't put my finger on it. I do know that Terry was awake also...I did have a vision in the third eye that resembled Dad ... I stayed awake awhile, eventually falling back to sleep.

Woke up with the same reality as the past six weeks. Ben is no longer in the physical world. Such a huge concept to grasp. Received an email from my friend, Nancy, stating that she knows this week will be a tough one and that she is sending her thoughts and prayers. Very kind gesture and beautiful friend. But one thing I realize in this newly established position as a grieving parent is that every day is a tough one! There are some worse than others, but overall, to date, they have each been a tough day to get through. The only thing that could change anything would be waking up after being incoherent for weeks to realize it was actually a bad dream and that Ben's suicide never happened.

But it did.

Everything I do now, routine things like taking an hour for a walk or getting on the treadmill, is an effort. And everything I manage to do is an accomplishment.

My sis-in-law, Steph Cullen, stopped by around 10:30 a.m. to drop off a gift for our family and stayed to visit for a couple hours. It was very nice to share feelings of despair, confusion, anger, and the many emotions that come with losing a child. Who better to understand than another parent also grieving the absence of their child? Steph lost her five-year-old daughter, Abby, to myocarditis.

One comment that I hear often is how suicide survivors seem to struggle for years after the suicide occurred. While different circumstances factor into each death, there are also similarities. What I do know is that survivors can either sink or swim. It is my desire to swim and help others as well. Faith in God will ensure this happens.

An experience that has happened to me several times since Ben's death is the desire to jump from the car as someone is driving it. Other feelings of frustration and anger have surfaced when I find myself using unacceptable vocabulary. I'm unsure why cursing has become frequent, since I haven't used such words for some time, nor do I feel they are acceptable even at this awful time. But they just come out. Another sensation I've had is to throw my cell phone against anything where it could smash into pieces. It's happened several times, though I've so far managed to stop myself from destroying my phone.

More than 20 of us attended the SOS meeting in Madison tonight, all of us looking for advice on how to get through the holidays without our loved ones who took their lives by suicide. Our family noticed the representation in attendance of those having lost young males who took their lives—sons, brothers, grandsons. Clearly suicide impacts both females and males, but based on the families' representation at SOS meetings, it appears suicide has a stronger impact on young males. Our family contributed to the discussion, and as class wrapped up, participants shared a message or comment that resonated with them. Four of those came from me. One of them was that nobody can understand the sadness a mother experiences losing a child. We carried them in our womb for nine months and have a bond like no other. Another appreciated how "tears of love" is how I express my emotions. I have cried so much for Ben. On the way home, I told Carrie about wanting to jump from the car or smash my cell phone. Carrie explained that these feelings are normal and represent my need to find things I can control while other aspects of life have spun out of control. Carrie suggested going to a thrift store and purchasing plates for a "ceremony" with our family where we would throw the plates on the ground to remove some anger. She also suggested activities like running on the treadmill versus walking and other physical activities that would alleviate feelings of stress, frustration, etc. This youngest child of mine astonishes me with her fortitude.

1/5/2015

I am struggling with people who think they know what's best for me right now because I don't even know that. How can they think they do? What I do know is that Ben's death affects our family directly and at a magnitude only God can understand. Just because it will make others feel better to see us back in our daily routines to give them a sense of normalcy, Ben's death and suicide have had a drastic impact, and we will be forever changed. For those who have not had this cross to bear, we only ask that you respect the trials of our journey and give us the time and space needed in our efforts to process this. It may take a lifetime.

1/6/2015

I decided to walk on the treadmill for a second day this week with the nudge of Ben. As I walked, I wept, praying to God, Jesus, Ben, Dad, Greg, Abby, grandparents, and all in spirit who will listen and come to the aid of our family to please help us through this pain. I attempted to compose myself so I could do some reading to aid in healing. As I did, thirty minutes into it, I heard crying. I looked to the doorway of the exercise room, and there stood Carrie, God help us, after sobbing her eyes out.

After a night with little sleep, I was feeling extremely vulnerable and tired. I headed to Bonnie's for reflexology and Reiki this morning. It's helping tremendously. Bonnie is a gifted, beautiful woman. I am grateful our paths crossed during this lifetime. She has been a GODSEND through my mourning, and her energy healing is truly helping me. As suggested by Bonnie, I recently found a recording she did, and I listened to it again. I found it very interesting to be reminded of where I was emotionally at the time and how the message she'd shared with me then resonated with me now, but even more so because of how Ben was feeling. I felt reassured that things are going to change and that goodness will come from Ben's tragedy. I left Harmony House at 12:15 p.m. and arrived home to find Terry there. He had cried all morning at work and had to leave. Terry realized that maybe it was too soon or too difficult to return to work, so he decided to take the rest of this week off and try again next Monday.

My boss had called while I was at Harmony House and then sent a text saying I needed to get back to her. I explained the day I was having and that it wasn't a good time to chat. I returned her call when I got back home and was feeling more stable. She was insistent that I commit to returning to work on Monday the 12th. After expressing that I could not, she said then paperwork would need to be completed with regard to the Family Medical Leave Act. I asked her to mail this information, and again she was insistent that I stop by the bank, as her text also stated, by 4:00 p.m. Carrie and I stopped by, and my boss met me at the bank door exit with an envelope, and I thanked her.

While we were driving, Mandy called. She had just started a nanny position with a new family. When they asked if she enjoyed the holidays, Mandy explained that her brother had passed. They expressed their condolences and shared that their nephew, Ben, had also passed. Mandy asked them to repeat their nephew's name, which they confirmed was Ben. He was 27...the same age as Beno, except their nephew died from cancer. Interesting how correlations present themselves that give us reminders that Ben is still around us by giving these signs. Another pretty exhausting day for all of us, but we got through it.

1/7/2015

I had an 8:00 a.m. medical appointment with my doctor so I could get the Family Medical Leave Act form signed and returned to the bank in hopes that work would leave me alone during the rest of my mourning. I still wanted to dodge the gal at the front desk since she acted oblivious during my last visit. Incredible how such a know-it-all person would not be aware of our misfortune when the rest of the office knew of it and showed kindness. I realized she doesn't owe me anything, but her lack of concern or expression of sympathy shocked me, especially when she has known our family for years. I need to get past being pissed by people's ignorance, but that's just where I'm at right now. Of course, as I enter the building, guess who is working? Yep! I avoid her and go stand behind a person that another worker is waiting on. She beckons me. I think she's enjoying this. Or maybe it's just me being highly sensitive and emotional these days. She asks for an emergency contact, saying they need one. Hmmm...Ben was previously listed as my emergency contact—another opportunity for her to possibly acknowledge his death...nope! Some people are just idiots to me at this point...and I apologize for having these feelings, I really do. Some people just don't know how to act or what to say. I get that, I really do, because I feel the same way at times. But what I do know is sometimes no words are needed, and a hug goes a long way.

At the doctor's office, I didn't spend much time in the waiting room, thank goodness. Nurse Paula called my name, and after weighing me in, she escorted me into a room and we visited. What a wonderful soul, providing support and comfort with regard to Ben's death. Paula was also very reassuring of our position and election to take the time needed before returning to work. She expressed her deepest sympathy for us having to go through this tragedy, saying she couldn't even imagine it. She and I spent forty-five minutes together and shared laughter and tears. What a kind person. I truly appreciated her genuine concern and care. The doctor came in next, and I repeated, to some extent, my earlier conversation, but this time with the doctor being an active listener who offered great support for our situation. The doctor shared her concerns with the stigma of suicide and how it can affect anyone.

The doctor stated that she has another client who is a father struggling with his child being on antidepressants. This father thinks his daughter should be able to manage on her own without taking meds. I couldn't believe it! Are there people out there who would rather have their child end up dead?! The doctor reassured the father that it is crucial that his daughter take these meds since her brain does not function like his, which is why she needs help to deal with the feelings and issues she has. This doctor of mine isn't a pill pusher, yet she validates concern for her patients. She also understands the stigma of suicide.

She compared it to the situation of a male middle-aged patient with diabetes. She suggested he take his meds, change his diet, exercise, and avoid drinking and smoking. He ignored her advice and ended up dying of a heart attack. People viewed his death as a tragedy when, in essence, he elected to end his life knowingly by not making certain changes, and the inevitable occurred.

Why is it when a person gets cancer or diabetes or any other health condition, action is encouraged, while mental health issues are viewed as weaknesses, and the encouragement is subtle at best? Why?! I doubt any person comes into the world asking to have a mental health condition. People need to be educated to understand that mental health conditions are common, and when they do occur, action should be taken and support should be given.

I asked the doctor if she would be a contact going forward in our efforts to educate others on mental health, and she agreed to help. She is wonderful! After my appointment, I went to Harmony House to see Bonnie. I love her. She has done so much for me during this time of mourning. After reflexology came Reiki, as usual. There was so much going on during this session, I can't even recall everything. I felt Ben's presence immediately when Bonnie started. At one point, I recalled a vision of a man's cheeks with whiskers. I couldn't figure out who the man was because I didn't see all his facial features. I looked for the chin to see if it had a cleft in it, knowing that would represent Ben, but the rest of the face never manifested. I did sense it may have been my dad. At another point, I saw the light of what a spirit represents to me. Next, a heart appeared in the center of the beautiful colors of purple and blue. These visions disappeared as quickly as they came. Next, I was looking down over someone. I saw the transformation of a face appear as if it was being created by a printer from the top of the head to the chin. As this vision was produced, I realized it was Ben! It disappeared immediately. Next, I felt as if someone had a paintball gun and was throwing the color green toward me. It was pretty intense. I knew this was Archangel Raphael sending healing into me. The appointment was incredible. I shared the experience with Bonnie afterward, which made us both happy. When I got home, I worked on the checkbook and spent some time journaling. At 3:30, Terry and I headed to the movie theater to see American Sniper with Bradley Cooper. The show must have been close to being sold out. The movie was incredible and gave me an appreciation for our veterans and what they go through to keep us free. I realized that everyone has their crosses to bear. To that statement, we shouldn't judge others, since we don't know the path they've walked.

2/20/2015

I woke up sleepy, but that happens. I decided I'd go into work early and leave once I got in a half day. Before going, I talked to Carrie for a while. She had some things to share, and I know I need to be a better listener for her. Carrie and Matt had talked about Ben's death. She wanted Matt to express his feelings, which weren't apparent, and this frustrated her. Matt wished that he would have gotten to know Ben better; he was upset with seeing the sadness that Ben's death has left on our family. Carrie shared her own realizations that she hasn't been able to deal with Ben's death to the extent I have. She knew that I was still experiencing Greg, Dad, and other family members' deaths in addition to Ben's. Even after a three-month leave from work, I was still trying to deal with this new reality.

Carrie had graduated college from the University of Minnesota at the time of Ben's suicide and was living at home to prepare for her move to Corning, New York, to partake in an AmeriCorps experience. Mandy had recently moved back to Wisconsin from living in Colorado and ended up in the AmeriCorps program in Madison. When Ben was living in La Crosse, this was the closest proximity our family had been in for a long time. Carrie shared that, at times, the impact of comments and conversations takes its toll on her. She typically puts a smile on her brave face and conjures up the strength to get through each day. Hearing Carrie was important because I doubt that she imposes on others with her feelings, and I don't want her carrying the weight of Ben's death without the support she needs. It was 7:30 a.m. when I headed to work. I felt ready to take on the day. Once inside my office, I noticed a plaque that had been placed on my credenza. It was a gift from the personal bankers that read, "When it hurts to look back and you're afraid to look ahead, look beside you, and there will be your friends." Needless to say, I wept and then read the beautiful card they'd each written a personalized message in, and I wept more.

I needed a hug in the worst way, but the only person at work at the time was Pete, and I figured if I walked into his office asking for a hug, he'd say, "That's not in my job description." I shouldn't judge, though, because I never gave him the chance to react to my request. I went downstairs to retrieve another box of Kleenex in the coat room. As I reached for a box of tissues, Jenni walked in to hang up her coat. As she did, I asked if I could get a hug, which she agreed to after she removed her coat. We embraced even as I continued to weep; I felt comforted.

Deanne came in as Jenni left, and she, in turn, offered a hug while I wept and drew comfort from her embrace. I did find the courage later in the morning to make my way downstairs to thank each of the ladies who gave me the plaque. Needless to say, there were many tears shed but also many hugs given and received. That's what gives me strength to go on. I also acknowledged my own strength for the effort and energy it took to make my way back in the view of many. It gave me a sense of such accomplishment and victory. I realized coming back to work is going to take time for me to adjust to.

Had a wake at Melby Funeral Home this morning for Merlyn, a lifelong neighbor and family friend. I have been to more funerals in the past four months than I care to think about. Afterward, Terry and I picked up the girls and headed out to his folks' house. I was anxious to see how his mom, Pat, was doing since getting home last week after open heart surgery. Terry's siblings had pictures from our niece Erin's recent destination wedding, which took place the day before Ben's birthday. Thirty or forty family members made the trip to join in the celebration. Looking through pictures, I reflected, knowing that we won't experience the happiness of Benjamin's wedding.

It was nice to see everyone, and I'm thankful that Pat is recovering so well. Looking at this 83-year-old woman, you'd never know she had open heart surgery less than a week ago. We stayed and visited until after lunch. When we got home, the family thought naps were in order. I decided I wanted to go to the thrift shop and purchase glass plates to aid in the therapy of smashing them and releasing some bottled-up feelings. Pam rode with me to make my purchase. Didn't feel like today was the day for plate smashing, but at least I have the plates. Now to decide on a location where I can do this without an audience who might pass judgment on my actions. I'll wait for another day.

Being spontaneous, Pam and I headed from Lancaster to Dubuque to continue our shopping excursion. Upon arriving, I got a text from Mandy asking my whereabouts. Apparently she, Carrie, and Terry just finished washing and cleaning out Carrie's car. A hand car wash in the driveway was something Terry and Ben bonded over during many of Ben's trips *home. Ben liked his car spotless; it was his pride and joy. Terry and the girls decided to stop by the Badger Bar Saloon for a beer. They wanted to have a cookout at our house after leaving the tavern. Everyone was lit like a Christmas tree. While I was happy they had enjoyed their day, I felt somewhat of an outcast, which made me miss Ben more.*

4/6/2015

Wow, this day was a challenge from the beginning to the end. I decided to take a walk and passed the former Gray Elementary School. I could imagine our kids playing on the playground. Tears started to flow, and I couldn't seem to contain them for most of the day. My heart longed for Benjamin so badly.

At work, I shared a story a few times with those who asked about our Easter. I told them how our family heard the song "Come as You Are" and how the girls and I wept, and I did my best to console them. I also told them about our trip to the cemetery with flowers and candy. Later, I resorted to unbagging Ben's blanket for smells that reminded me of him. I did have an appointment with Bonnie after work ... again, much needed. I entered in tears and left feeling peace and tranquility. Bonnie reassured me that healing is taking place, and I agree with her completely.

4/7/2015

Returned to work for a full day today. A coworker made the comment during a conversation, "Well, as long as you feel you're making progress." This pissed me off to no end. Someone who has never been in this position cannot begin to imagine what our family is going through. I didn't appreciate her feelings of judgment and doubt she can begin to understand what it feels like to lose a child. There are lots of judges out there who think they have it all figured out. I am not sure how they know what's best for me when I haven't even figured that out for myself. Thank God I had an appointment with Bonnie at Harmony House after work. It was much needed. Mandy came home after her first day at her new job and joined Terry, Carrie, Matt, and I for a cookout. Had dinner while watching the Badgers basketball team; they gave it a run for their money, but, in the end, lost the championship game.

The quest for reasons why Ben allowed this to happen never ceases for me. I know this is a commonality for survivors. I pray as each survivor moves forward through their individual journey that they move at a pace that is doable for them. For those of you who haven't had to endure such a loss, I pray you will offer grace and patience as you interact with those who have.

※

She speaks wise words and teaches others to be kind.
Proverbs 31:26 (NCV)

CHAPTER 5

INVESTIGATION AND REASONING

There is a way that seems right to a man, but its end is the way of death.
Proverbs 14:12 (NKJV)

As much as my investigative mind tries to understand when Benjamin made the lone decision to take his life, how he chose the method in doing so, and why that date and time, I am very well aware that the answers I seek will not be answered. And more importantly, even if they were, it won't bring Ben back. But it does leave me perpetually spinning into...

PHASE 3: INVESTIGATION AND REASONING

When I look back at the emails I saved from my last exchange with Ben, no apparent red flags came to me. At the time, I didn't pause to wonder if there was anything out of the ordinary with him, and because of this, I do carry the guilt that I failed Ben as his mom.

1/14/2015

Walked the treadmill again while reading; I also said my daily prayers. Mandy called in the morning and was quite upset about Ben. We talked for fifteen minutes or so while she expressed her concerns, trying to understand the reasoning for Ben's decision. We can all speculate and possibly rule out things, but I'm not certain we will ever get all the answers to the questions we have. Terry made it through his third day at work. I returned to Harmony House for additional energy healing.

Meghan came over for another meeting with us. We played "Come as You Are," a song that was played at Ben's funeral, and I called Barbara, who works with a depression and suicide support group in Green Bay, for advice about starting a group in our area. That evening, Terry and I attended an SOS meeting. There are always newcomers each week, so suicide isn't going away. Had a large group, so we decided to divide up into two groups for the session. One of those present had lost their loved one who was a mother of three. She had a wonderful husband, was doing well financially, and seemed emotionally stable. It appeared she was living a great life until she took her own life. Her friends searched up and down trying to uncover the reasons for this act, but they were left without answers. Sometimes we won't know the reasoning but will have to come to terms with that as we move forward. Seeing other survivors in the group gives us hope that, in time, we will feel happiness again. I hope and pray for this.

I kept waking up during the night, and Terry left for work in the middle of the night. I grabbed a notebook and pen off of Terry's end table and scribbled in the dark the thoughts that were coming to mind. First, I have been hearing music a lot since Ben died. Initially, for the first two weeks, I heard music both day and night in my mind. It played whenever I was idle. Lately, I've heard music playing again. The message I'm hearing is that I need to dance again … in life. I'm confident it will aid in finding the joy I so desire. I also was guided to focus on making memories in our new reality versus avoiding it. While it is OK to reflect on old memories with fondness and admiration, I should not consume myself with sadness. I went back to sleep at 6:00 a.m., only to wake up at 7:00 to give Carrie a hug and wish her well with her new duties today.

Then I returned to bed and lay awake thinking of Ben, feeling depths of pain and the sadness of missing him. I concluded that the levels of this pain are to give me some sense of how lonely and sad Ben may have felt. *The thought even crossed my mind that if I feel this sad, who would miss me if I were gone? It appears others are getting on with their lives just fine while my life has stalled. There are good moments, of course. But the hole in my heart reminds me daily of our enormous loss and that Benjamin is no longer on this earth with us.*

Ben just couldn't have thought ahead to know what he was leaving behind. One contemplating suicide may not think that far ahead or about that. It's unfortunate because if they could see a preview, they'd see what's left for others to deal with. Tremendous despair, unanswered questions and feelings of guilt, shame, and sadness for failing to know, for failing to save them.

Mom picked me up at 10:00 a.m. We went to Dickeyville for breakfast before traveling on to Sinsinawa to walk the labyrinth. Spent some time meditating and waiting to receive messages. A big part of today is for me to realize that I cannot dwell in this sorrow forever. I think of Dad. When he was ill, I loved him enough to let him go. I need to look at Ben's death this way too, but it is a much easier thought to let go of someone you love and miss so much than to actually do it.

Ben didn't have the quality of life that he desired, and now he is at peace. Whether I like it or not, this is our new reality. And the sooner I accept this, the sooner I can go forward versus reeling in such despair and sadness each day. While I want to acknowledge efforts I've taken to heal through this grief, I pray for the day that I see goodness from all this pain. One thing I've wished over and over again is to turn back time so Ben could still be here. I think it's more that I wish Ben would have been honest with us on how he was feeling. How do you help someone struggling if they don't ask for help? I feel betrayed at times, like I didn't know who Ben was. I mean, we did know Ben, but only what he shared with us. Obviously, he didn't share his deepest, truest feelings. Why? We know from his suicide letter he didn't want to burden us. I'm guessing that he also didn't want to show weakness or failure or sadness, so it was easiest to avoid sensitive topics at all costs. And comparing, I think Ben looked at others and felt less than because he hadn't accomplished what others had or thought he should have at this point in his life. Unfortunately, I believe it contributed to Ben's death.

1/15/2015

Had an appointment with Bonnie today at Harmony House at 10:00 a.m. I'm taking care of myself and need to prepare for getting back into the routine of life and the workforce. I realized there were no checks in the checkbook, so I decided to use an ATM machine to get cash to pay Bonnie. In the drive-through at the bank, the eyes of the cashier widened, and she asked how I was. I replied that I was hanging in there as tears welled up in my eyes. I cried on my way to Harmony House and was embraced by Bonnie with a warm hug. We talked for forty-five minutes before she performed reflexology and Reiki.

I came home to find Terry in our kitchen after a rough time at work. He had left work at 11:30 a.m. We struggle daily to determine how we can go forward in our lives without Ben. He couldn't have considered how badly he would be missed by so many and the despair his family would be in. We pray for the day we'll have a more in-depth, spiritual relationship with our son.

Spent time in the afternoon contacting the Onalaska Police Department, the La Crosse County chief medical examiner, RTI Donor Services, and Gundersen Health System, requesting reports and medical records ... again. Just speaking to strangers, professionals that they are, about Ben's death eats me up inside. I feel like this subject is one I need to accustom myself to whether I like it or not. And it doesn't get any easier each time it's discussed. How does the reality of your loved one dying by suicide get easier, or how do you learn to live with this? Is it possible?

2/4/2015

I survived another day. I even heard the song from Ben's funeral while Ashley was visiting me at my desk at work. I held it together and didn't break down. Tried to reflect on goodness and fond memories. Worked all day, but as I left to walk home that night, I realized that even if I bury my tears, they will come. I cried all the way home.

I also realized how some of the most important people in my life are now in spirit. I know they are at peace. I pray I find peace in all of this too. Have been wanting to call and talk with Connie, the school superintendent again. She's a suicide-survivor mom … she gets it! I have also thought about forming a mom's group and getting together with some of these gals more frequently. Maybe I'll bring it up at the next SOS group meeting we have next week. The weekend of Memorial Day 2015, we were invited to a 40th birthday celebration, and Terry and I decided to go. As we were driving Ben's car on rural County Highway O, I got the urge to use the bathroom. Couldn't think of a place to find a potty, which I'd need in this case. Then we realized our friends, Tim and Lisa, had a place in that neck of the woods. As we drove down the lane to their home, a red cardinal swept directly in front of the car's windshield. Terry and I both commented on it. It's a well-known belief that a red cardinal symbolizes a visit from a spirit.

After we pulled into Tim and Lisa's, I got out and knocked on their door. Lisa answered, pleasantly surprised. I told her my dilemma and asked about using the restroom, and, of course, she obliged. She asked where Terry was and went out to the car to invite him in. We ended up staying there a few hours. The night was calm, and the conversation flowed with lots of laughter and tears. We were confident that there was a reason Terry suggested taking County O to Potosi and that the cardinal was a sign from Ben that we needed to be with these friends at that time. Even though we didn't get to the birthday dinner, the therapy we received from our visit made us understand that we had been guided to their house that evening. We were where we were supposed to be.

It still breaks my heart now knowing that the comments Ben made about his feelings were much deeper than we ever realized. I'm so sorry, Ben. I wish I would have been a better listener and not assumed that your position was something I thought I was familiar with or something we'd gone through with the girls before. My heart breaks daily for assuming this.

What I do know is that as much as I thought our family had great communication skills, being an active listener takes on much more seriousness now.

At this month's SOS meeting, we had twelve attendees, three being new participants. It is incredible for me to hear the stories and see the sadness that resides in others who have experienced loss due to suicide. Many of these folks carry their pain for so many years. I am thankful for the brave participants who venture into SOS to share their stories with tears and emotions. I pray that together we may all heal and find our way to memories that bring us comfort over sadness as we move forward on our journeys.

I also experienced my first appointment with a psychologist. I didn't have any expectations and really wasn't sure why I was going. Guess my doctor thought this guy may be able to help me with post-traumatic stress disorder (PTSD). I shared heart-wrenching memories and pain from the night of the suicide. While I wept uncontrollable tears, this gentleman sat across the room from me, nodding his head. There weren't many words on his part, which I guess only makes sense since he needs to hear my story to better understand my reasoning for being there and to determine the best way to help me. As the hour came to an end, he suggested an exercise for me. He asked me to close my eyes, take a few deep breaths, and envision a box with a chute on it. This box is where I could store any images, thoughts, emotions, feelings, etc. When I feel ready, I can retrieve these items and deal with them. He then asked me to secure the box. I envisioned a vault being placed over a casket, which was very upsetting to me. He apologized for this visual and had me take a couple deep breaths. Then I closed my eyes. As I did, I could literally envision myself sitting on a hillside with my knees pulled up and hands hugging my knees. As I looked out, I could see water with the sun shining on it and a long pier with the box floating in front. I felt a sense of peace and comfort. As I left an hour and fifteen minutes later, I decided to schedule another appointment and see where this experience in therapy goes.

6/7/2015

Derek asked to wear Ben's graduation gown for his graduation ceremony, which we agreed to. However, the ceremony was just around the corner, and he still hadn't picked it up. We decided to deliver it. I

went first, and Terry came over shortly behind me with gown in hand.
Pam called Derek in to retrieve the gown. There weren't many words
exchanged at that time. Later, I heard about Derek's frustration as he
was working on a video to be played at his graduation party. Then Bruce
shared that while Derek was working downstairs on the video, he played
a loud song over and over again that reminded him of Ben. Close cousins
as they were, it sank in how much Derek missed Ben too.

Bruce stated how these actions by Derek made it almost impossible for
him to not break down in tears. Pam said when Derek went upstairs to
get ready for graduation, he played the song loudly again. We all knew
that while there was reason to celebrate, there was also a missing link
that everyone felt in their gut and their heart. That's what some might
not understand. Just because there is a happy moment doesn't mean it
isn't accompanied by sadness, and this is an example of that. At Derek's
graduation ceremony, Terry and I sat in the bleacher section above the
floor where Pam, Bruce, Mom, Mandy, and the graduates sat. As the
students entered the gymnasium, Derek made his entrance. I could see
that Terry was getting choked up. I couldn't focus on that or I would fall
apart. Instead, I looked proudly at Derek and what a fine young man our
godson had grown into as we celebrated this huge milestone.

 **7/1/2016:** I took a road trip with Barb. I love my friend so much. We enjoyed lunch at Quivey's Grove in Fitchburg before going to Karen's Rock Shop. We had limited time to shop, but I found myself returning to a malachite rock with a rough exterior and smooth, dipped interior, which I purchased. I didn't realize something about it until we were traveling home and I looked down into the stone. As I was running my thumb over it, I noticed what appeared to be a figure of a male. He appeared to be kneeling and praying. Intuitively, I felt it was Ben and heard audibly, "Forgive me so you can heal your heart." Barb noticed the aura around the head of the figure, and I then noticed it was around its entire body. A heart outlined this figure when I looked at it from

either the top or bottom. There was also a source of power represented as God to me that encompassed the very exterior rim of the rock. It was incredible to think that the reason I purchased this rock was because of a connection I felt, then to see what the rock truly represented gave me a sense of transcendence. Our neighbor, Mary K., suggested that the ripples within the rock's pattern reflect our lives and the lives of others on this journey.

8/26/2016

It was Sunday morning, and the day of our vacation to Chetek was finally here! Terry and I finished packing the truck and boat. We attended church before venturing onward. Leave it to Pastor Mark to notice our boat outside the church and incorporate it into his morning message on how all of us are God's fishermen. He also recognized the importance of our desire to stop at church versus passing by. He could see that even with our excitement to get to our destination, taking a moment to praise God was important to us. Pastor Mark is a gift and has that effect. We look forward to his weekly Sunday message that aids us to move forward in life. The love of our church and the encouragement with acceptance Pastor offers makes life bearable, even in the most difficult circumstances when darkness can easily consume us. We give thanks for Pastor Mark. Upon exchanging hugs with others after church, we went onward to Chetek!

In hopes of making new memories, we avoided our usual resort since our last trip to Chetek was just weeks before Ben took his life. That in itself was one of the reasons for our hesitation in making this usual trip to Chetek. I am so grateful we allowed ourselves to return. We enjoyed our trip down memory lane and reflected on how life had once been, how it has changed, and how there are still many experiences to enjoy and memories to be made.

I already knew it was the start to an amazing vacation. We spent glorious days on the boat and fished all but one day. Terry cleaned the fish, and we stayed in and read the book Pastor Mark had given us. He offered two copies of The Gift of Encouragement, a book written by his brother John Dieter, on living powerfully through adversity. He knew this book would contribute to our healing journey, and it did! It also validated our growing belief that some of the lessons we learn are through others' experiences, which is one of the reasons for the writing of my book. I pray that Tears of Love casts light on your journey.

God offered many messages to me during our vacation. One came to me as I lay in bed that night after Terry and I had spent the afternoon fishing. For four hours, I watched Terry pull in fish after fish. I could not understand how we could be in the same boat, just a few feet apart, using the same bait and the same jig to fish, and he reeled in fish while I did not catch a single one. I was actually not upset about this, because I love to fish, and I enjoyed God's beauty all around me.

Not catching any fish was more enjoyable than working, but I wondered what this meant. Then I got it. I had always placed Dad and Benjamin on a pedestal, but where did Terry rank on this pedestal? Over our many years together, Terry had always provided for me and our family, and he continues to provide. In the past twenty-two months, not only has he contributed financially but also emotionally more than ever. I would not be here if it were not for his continued love and support, us working side-by-side through the loss of Benjamin. After thirty-three years of marriage, I have a new appreciation for the gift Terry is in my life and the love we share. I have moved him up on the pedestal as high as he can go, right below God and Jesus.

 12/22/2016: Carrie and I headed to Dubuque, and not surprisingly, the topic of Ben came up. I was having a rough day, missing him beyond words. Carrie reassured me that we can't change the past, we did the best we could, and Ben does not want us to be sad. She added that it hurts her heart when I do this to myself. I listened as I cried, then all of the sudden I heard "Angels Among Us" by Alabama, a song of the Christmas season. Carrie reassured me this was Ben's way of reminding us that he, Grandpa (my dad), Uncle Greg, Abby, Tom, Chris, Laura, and so many other loved ones we have lost are still with us in spirit.

 Carrie was in pursuit of a computer during this trip, one of our main reasons for going to Dubuque. It is always a bittersweet experience because Benjamin was our tech guy. He was so very tech-savvy, and not having his expertise has been a real challenge. As we walked into Best Buy, a young man walked up behind us almost immediately and asked how he could help us. At first it startled us, but then we realized that this nice young man named Richard (my deceased father's name) had the helpfulness and knowledge of Ben. He was so kind and even stayed an extra hour as Carrie pondered all the options he shared. This was another event filled with reminders that our loved ones are still with us. Not sure how you did that, God, but I definitely noticed and appreciated it. Thank you! God is good all the time...all the time...God is good.

2/14/2017

Valentine's Day. Definitely in a better mindset for work today compared to yesterday. I think I cried myself out for a few days, anyway. Not sure how I would have reacted yesterday, but I'm confident my mindset is in a much better place today. I received belated birthday wishes from my colleagues. Six of my pals entered my office later in the afternoon singing "Happy Birthday," which was so sweet. As I extended hugs to my friends for their kindness, support, and love, I shared with them the reasoning for staying away yesterday. I had actually contemplated stopping by the bank on my birthday, knowing my friends would have graciously offered hugs—which is what I draw strength from—but it didn't seem fair to disrupt their day by coming in and then leaving them with the sadness I was feeling. However, today I was able to express my hurting heart and sadness and despair of missing Ben. I also focused on the blessings and gifts my girls are to me. It was wonderful to spend Sunday with them. As

I thought of the girls, I found my heart heavy again, knowing that they were hurting and missing Benjamin so much. I wish there was something I could do to help ease their pain.

March 2018

Usually, we take a family trip over Ben's birthday, but because of upcoming expenses for the girls, Terry and I decided that this year it would be just the two of us spending time at a resort in Door County. We were elated about getting away and taking time to reflect. We packed a suitcase of clothes and another with books. En route to Door County, I received a text from my coworker who needed to talk. Her aunt and uncle lost their 24-year-old son to suicide in February and were struggling. I encouraged her to have her aunt call me at any time.

On our first night there, we met a group of kids as we entered the building. They were having a smoke break, and Terry was pushing a cart with all of our belongings. As we wheeled by them, they noticed we had brought some beer with us. They offered to take this off our hands. We laughed and shared that we were just starting our vacation and would probably have a few during our stay. Terry and I unpacked and then headed to Casey's BBQ & Smokehouse. We knew the weather was going to turn from cool to cold with snow predicted for the coming week. We enjoyed a beautiful lake sunset. Upon our return, we went to the front desk to check on times for church.

As we were making our way back to our room, we crossed paths with the young adults we'd met earlier. Their door was open, and when they saw us, they insisted we join them for a shot of tequila followed by a shot of pickle juice! We learned they were friends away on an annual getaway weekend. We shared our reasoning for vacationing over Ben's birthday and that he had taken his life. Then their stories started to spill out. Most of them had struggled and even contemplated suicide. Seems to be a common story of people we meet. We thanked them for sharing their stories, reassured them suicide is not the answer, commended their growth and continued efforts, and offered them BENS Hope bracelets with TheHopeLine information.

Later during our stay, Terry and I went into Sturgeon Bay for massages. While shopping in town, I was approached by the store clerk. Being in a tourist town, it was natural for her to ask where we were from and what brought us to the area. As we chatted, of course Ben's birth and death came up. This woman shared that she was a retired psychiatrist and currently worked on a hotline. She went on to say she'd talked with many people and even had people take their lives while she was on the phone. I was a bit surprised when she shared, but I believed I was exactly where I was supposed to be for her to offer this insight and share her heart, thoughts, and feelings with me. I was thankful for her trust and comfort and hope. It allowed her to lighten the weight she may have been carrying from these experiences stemming from her career as support on the hotline.

We finally arranged a long visit with my coworker Lexie's aunt and uncle, Pat and Diane, who have recently lost their son to suicide. Their brokenness was apparent, and our hearts ached knowing the journey that awaited them. We offered to pray with them, but they said they weren't there yet in their faith. I reassured them it was OK and that we would continue to pray for them. We know by the grace of God that this is the reason we are still holding it together, healing, and moving forward. But we also appreciate that each person has their own unique journey to figure things out. And we respect this completely.

3/9/2018

We had plans to meet up with the girls for an overnight stay. Mandy hosted us at her place in Madison. Carrie was already there when we arrived later in the afternoon. First on the agenda was an update on Carrie and Matt's wedding. Sounds like the kids are considering moving their wedding from a barn venue to a place closer to home. Mandy took us to a quaint pub after, then pizza. It was the most enjoyable and lighthearted gathering we'd shared in some time. Evenings like this and our other social events are important to us. But we have to work them around getting to church, which is important to us. Church refuels us each week and has become a top priority.

3/12/2018

Anxiety set in as I looked at the week ahead. I had medical appointments for a kidney stone, a counseling appointment, an SOS meeting, Bible study, and Lent services. I had started reading an intriguing book by Anne Graham Lotz, which I cannot recall at the moment, but what I do recall is that I didn't want to put this book down. As it drew closer for me to get ready for work, I heard God speak. He was telling me that I needed a "me" day. I shrugged it off the first time I heard it. But He was persistent. How could I stay home? I had been out all last week in Door County, had only worked Monday, took off Tuesday afternoon for appointments, and was going to be out Thursday to attend a mental health meeting! Should I stay home today? It didn't make sense. I had delayed things long enough! It was time to get ready for work! But as I turned the page, the words I read were actual words I say often but do not hear from others. I read, "There are 60 seconds in a minute and 60 minutes in an hour." My jaw dropped! I felt as though God was speaking to me through Anne's book. This gave me validation that I was supposed to stay home and read this book. Next thing I knew, I was texting work saying I would not be in. Little did I know what the day would bring!

I continued reading Anne's book. The more I read, the more consumed I became. The words spoke to my heart. I was literally in the book! I became emotional as the words came to life! In the midst of my reading, I was guided to get a piece of paper and light a candle next to the 11x14 picture of Jesus on my coffee table. As I sat on the floor in front of my coffee table, I was guided to write down what was weighing heavy on my heart. This included actions by myself or others that called for forgiveness.

My pen could hardly keep up with the thoughts that were flooding through my mind—events that cycled back to my youth. As I wrote, tears fell from my eyes. After I completed writing, I was guided to read the words from the paper aloud. I wept. Tears flowed as I read each sentence, and my heart overflowed as I heard, "I forgive you," or, "You are forgiven." I could hear God's loving words of forgiveness and feel His love. I was guided to take the piece of paper outside, light it on fire, and let those sins go. I had professed them, and God had forgiven them. They need not be *rehashed again. Words cannot describe the weight that was lifted from my shoulders. Burdens from years gone by that were buried deep within my heart were released. These were wounds I'd covered up, made excuses for, or felt I deserved. I felt free, actually weightless. Interestingly, while I'd experienced emotional healing, even the physical pain I'd felt prior to this exercise ceased.*

As I went back into the house, I felt that the physical, mental, and emotional pains I'd been carrying were washed away. What an incredible healing experience.

If we confess our sins, He is faithful and just to forgive us our sins,
and to cleanse us from all unrighteousness.
1 John 1:9 (KJV)

I set an alarm on the microwave to allow enough time to prepare food for Terry's lunch break. When he came home, I was excited to share what had transpired. I explained that I felt God wanted me to stay home for a reason. There was so much happening with healing and reading and feelings. I knew God had orchestrated this day and time for me. I shared with Terry that I felt the book needed to be read prior to our speaking engagement coming up at UW-Platteville on behalf of the Clarity Clinic fundraiser. I felt it had something to do with our presentation. After Terry left for work, I returned to reading. A few minutes into my reading, the book referenced a cord of three strands, the theme for our speaking engagement hosted by the Clarity Clinic. Truly, it was a day to remember and an experience to share with others to aid in their healing and knowledge of our amazing and powerful God!

Later in 2018

One of our regular attendees at SOS lost her son twelve years ago. Her husband has never been to a meeting nor does he wish to talk about this loss. She says her husband's reasoning is that he may break down and doesn't want to share his pain publicly. This year, after the names were read at the annual BENS Hope 5K/2M event and the balloons were released, she turned around to see him there. What a blessing and an opportunity to start dealing and healing!!

After losing a loved one to suicide, we are left with a number of unanswered questions. Even once you receive an investigation report, coroner's report, or whatever report you await, you are left with questions. I have found no one who has had all their questions answered. I pray as you work through your loss and all the logistics that accompany it that you find the strength to move forward, one step at a time. Please know that baby steps are still steps moving forward.

And I say this because I am doing this myself, one step at a time. I recall a meditation I was doing on April 5, 2020. I started in prayer before resting in God's love and listening to Him. God said I need to forgive and that I am holding on to guilt. Ben's death was a suicide; I'm acting as if it was a homicide. I'm not guilty. Whether Ben called the day before or week before, he made the lone decision to take his life. I had reached out throughout the day of his death without a response from him. Ben knew I was there for him and how much love I had for him. God said I needed to release this burden to free myself and move forward and live with true joy in my life again. He desires this for me and our family. If you're a believer, I hope you know this. If you're not, I pray you will be curious to seek God out and receive His strength and never-ending love.

Trust in the Lord with all your heart and
do not lean on your own understanding.
Proverbs 3:5 (ESV)

CHAPTER 6

IDENTITY

I can do all things through God who strengthens me.
Philippians 4:13 (NKJV)

While my blessings are innumerable, which I thank God for daily, I've also had my share of losses. Because of these, I have worked through grief numerous times and have learned the importance of dealing with these feelings in order to heal. My faith has also guided me through my grief and greatly influenced my identity as the person I am today and the mission I'm on.

When I was 19 years old, my youngest brother, Greg, who turned 14 years old on September 21, 1981, was killed just four days later on September 25 in an automobile accident. Needless to say, this tragedy devastated my family and left us wondering how to move forward. There were days when it seemed impossible. But as society expects, we jump back on the merry-go-round of life, still broken and without healing. Because grief wasn't really talked about then and still isn't a topic of choice in today's world, I dealt with this loss the best way I could—drinking with my sister or friends. As hard as I tried to escape the reality of Greg's death and the feelings that accompany a loss, it became apparent that this coping mechanism only offered brief moments of relief; it all prominently returned the following day. I had the desire to talk with someone, anyone, actually, but whom? I didn't want to burden my parents; I knew they were already suffering.

Others didn't really ask or desire to talk about it. Needless to say, it was a sorrowful time.

I also lost my paternal grandparents, Walter and Anna, when I was very young. I recall that after my grandfather had passed, my elementary teacher asked what his name was. My reply was, "Grandpa." I recall her smiling at my response. I didn't realize my grandparents had names! And in 1987, I lost my feisty maternal grandma Mary soon after Ben was born.

In 1990, during my pregnancy with our youngest, Carrie, my maternal grandpa, John, passed away. Terry's godmother Marilyn also died from cancer. While both were adults, their losses were unexpected and painful.

Then tragedy struck again.

On April 28, 1990, we learned our 15-year-old nephew, Chris, was killed. He was a passenger on a dirt bike. The news hit me like a tidal wave as I relived the anguish of Greg's death. Later in counseling, I learned his loss was a trigger for me. Triggers that occur in the present can transport us back to traumatic events in our past, causing pain, emotional distress, flashbacks, or panic attacks. Six years later came another horrific loss. Our nephew, Tom, was involved in an automobile accident outside the city limits. His vehicle left the road that cold, snowy night, the scene obscured by a bridge, undetected until morning. Tom died on December 19, 1996. He was 19. Ten years later, another tragedy struck. On August 27, 2006, our beautiful niece, Laura, a passenger on a crotch rocket, was thrown off and died from her injuries. Laura, 20, was Tom's youngest sister. Words couldn't explain the devastation, but there was still more to come.

On December 20, 2009, as we eagerly awaited the homecoming of our children with the joy and anticipation the Christmas season brings, we received an early-morning phone call. It was Terry's mom, who was crying hysterically. I listened as she attempted to explain the situation between her sobs. We eventually learned our five-year-old little niece, Abby, had died. Another shock to everyone. Abby had flu-like symptoms over the weekend and passed unexpectedly. We would later learn that she died from myocarditis. Precious Abby was buried two days before Christmas. Another excruciating loss for the family.

Four months later, on April 13, 2010, my dad passed away at age 69 on the day before his 70th birthday. I'm not sure about you, but it's said that fathers are a son's first hero and a daughter's first love. My dad was definitely that. I still miss him every day.

And obviously while these weren't our only losses, never would death touch us so deeply as it did on November 11, 2014, a day that turned into a gut-wrenching, agonizing nightmare. It was a day that would cause such devastation; our family would never be the same again. The day was:

November 11, 2014

Veterans Day

the day that commemorates the service of all veterans

November 11

the date

forever engrained

the date

Ben chose

to take his life

and die

by suicide.

November 11, 2014, would become the day that would change the trajectory of our lives forever.

Our child's life ended at his own hand. And because of this, suicide has taken on a new, significant meaning in our lives and birthed a new mission. God put it on our hearts immediately to take action by sharing Ben's story. We agreed from the beginning that we would be honest about his death by suicide, and we wanted this truth to be known. Surviving the aftermath of Ben's decision is the most arduous work I have ever done. But we know this is not of our own doing. We don't have the capacity. I don't have the capacity. It's happening because of the faith we didn't know we had but have learned how much we needed.

Thinking back, I recall a particular statement I found myself reciting in multiple conversations. When others asked how I was doing, my rehearsed response was, "We're moving forward on our path one step at a time, lit by our love for Ben."

Imagine my surprise when I would later come across this scripture: *Your word is a lamp to guide my feet and a light for my path.* Psalm 119:105 (NLT)

This was another divine experience with God. I am thankful for His guidance and encouragement then, now, and always.

In the years since Ben left us, my encounters with other survivors have impacted me in a manner I didn't expect. God has guided us to speak to people and share our story, provide awareness, aid in prevention, offer support, and provide resources to reduce the stigma associated with suicide and mental health issues. We know more about suicide today than we ever wanted to. Because of our circumstances, it's on our hearts to help others. We want to be proactive and reassure others that there are a number of resources available for you or your loved ones. We want people to know they are not alone.

I would like to take this opportunity to acknowledge others who are also working to aid in suicide studies, promoting awareness and prevention, offering support, and so on. I admire all the work everyone is doing and feel it is truly a blessing having these resources and services available. Each of them is unique and offered with a valuable purpose and cause. Whether the American Foundation of Suicide Prevention (AFSP), the Jed Foundation, BENS Hope, Jacob's SWAG, the Suicide Prevention Corporation of Southwestern Wisconsin, the Center for Suicide Awareness in Kaukauna, the 988 Suicide and Crisis Lifeline, 741741—the Crisis Text Line, the U.S. National Suicide Prevention Lifeline at 800-273-TALK (8255) or others, there are many suicide-related resources available for you and your loved ones. Please familiarize yourself with these and utilize them to help yourself and others.

Losing Benjamin changed my purpose in this life and what I wished to do with the rest of my time in this world. But stepping into this new chapter would mean another significant loss—leaving my career at the bank: the place I grew up, the place that offered me security, and the place that had been my identity for over forty-three years.

I recall being recognized for my forty-year milestone. The Wisconsin Bankers Association hosted a lovely banquet with an elaborate dinner to bestow Lifetime Service Awards. As each name was announced, we made our way forward to receive a plaque for our tenure. While walking forth, an elected person spoke of each person's specific banking accomplishments. As I made my way toward the stage, I listened to my boss acknowledge my professional milestones, including our bank's growth, and other complimentary sentiments. As she did, I felt that tug in my heart and soul and found myself pondering: What do I want to do with the next years of my life? This was not a new thought. It was a constant one since Ben died, but this time, it penetrated my heart unlike ever before. And then I heard the response: do what God has been calling me to do, write *Tears of Love*, and help others who are struggling.

Sounds cut and dry, right? And I know it's in giving that we receive, but there were more questions. So where did I get answers to my questions? I turned to the Bible and found them.

In everything I did, I showed you that by this kind of hard work we must
help the weak, remembering the words the Lord Jesus Himself said:
"It is more blessed to give than to receive."
Acts 20:35 (NIV)

I know what it is to be in need, and I know what it is to have plenty. I have
learned the secret of being content in any and every situation, whether
well fed or hungry, whether living in plenty or in want.
Philippians 4:12 (NIV)

No one can serve two masters. Either you will hate the one and love the
other, or you will be devoted to the one and despise the other.
You cannot serve both God and money.
Matthew 6:24 (NIV)

Based on these scriptures, I am confident you can figure out the
questions I was asking God. While I fought with thoughts of leaving
the bank for eight years, it was becoming more apparent than ever at
this banquet that my time at the bank was drawing to a close. My eyes
were focused on a new feast.

But when you give a banquet, invite the poor, the crippled, the lame,
the blind, and you will be blessed. Although they cannot repay you,
you will be repaid at the resurrection of the righteous. When
one of those at the table with Him heard this, he said to Jesus,
"Blessed is the one who will eat at the feast in the kingdom of God."
Luke 14:13-15 (NIV)

As my journal entries continue, I share insight on struggles,
support, survival, and the blessings of giving and receiving. Even in
dire circumstances, these gifts were still prevalent.

12/25/2014

*Christmas. I survived. Many tears of love shed. I didn't know how we
would get through Christmas without Ben's presence, but somehow, we
managed. Christmas Eve was especially painful since Ben had been our
Santa's helper for years. Terry and I took time to do it this year since
Carrie specifically requested it. Mandy wasn't feeling the Christmas
spirit whatsoever. She'd said this whole thing wasn't right ... only having
her and Carrie opening presents instead of the three of them. My heart
hurts even more because she was hurting along with everyone else.*

1/5/2015

Rise and shine around 8 a.m. for breakfast. Terry and I needed to sneak off to Melby Funeral Home to attend a wake for Bob Osterholz, who died at 92 years of age. Once again, the nerves set in as we made our way there. Once inside, we realized there was a longer line than we expected. I realized a woman whom I've known and participated on committees and in events with stood ahead of us in line. As she noticed a presence behind her, she turned and realized it was us. She said hello and did a quick about-face. Intentional or not, it was another experience when I felt shunned from someone who knew me. It can't be described. Have you ever gone through this? It's as if you don't already feel enough despair for the loss you've endured and you've finally mustered the courage to make your way out of that dark depth of despair, only to encounter that you're on display and now have to deal with others' reactions to your presence. I finally have enough courage to make eye contact only to have others avoid me … ugh! It is not a fun situation to be in whatsoever. Don't they know that suicide is not contagious?

Fortunately, on this trip (our third funeral since Ben's) to Melby's Funeral Home, we saw my niece, Anna, having an especially rough day. I went over to her and attempted to comfort her, only to fall weak myself. Anna, in return, comforted me. My family is wonderful for this. We returned home and after lunch, I started reading, only to end up falling asleep. Naps seem to be more common these past few weeks. Without even knowing at times, I'll nod off for a short catnap. I figure they're needed and will get me through the rest of the day. When I woke up, Terry described our contributions toward the development of an SOS group. It's a step in the direction of creating a foundation in Ben's memory to help others who find themselves in the position we did.

2/9/2015

Mom and I went to The Dubuque Religious Center Inc., where I fell in love with bronze figurines of Archangels Raphael and Michael. I bought more books on grief to find hope and encouragement in the days that seem to be getting harder without Ben's presence. It's my desire to let go of this grief and celebrate our love for each other since we did share a deep love. God help me find comfort in the love we shared. After shopping, I went for my massage appointment at the salon, and the gals working gathered around me to ask how I was doing. I reassured them, and it was a reminder to myself that goodness will come from his death. Terry and I will ensure this. The massage was just what I needed—a full deep-tissue massage with little chatter and a full hour of peace and calm. During this time, my mind didn't wander. I wouldn't let it. I reminded myself not to live in the past or worry about the future but enjoy this present moment, which is exactly what I did. For this brief time, I felt like things would be alright. It was very encouraging.

2/11/2015

Woke up and walked on the treadmill for seventy minutes while talking with my friend, Sue. Very therapeutic! Took time afterward to say morning prayers; I'm much more significant and reflective these days since Ben's death. I give thanks for blessings and ask for guidance for our future. I realize only God knows the grander plan of this picture that we can't see clearly, but I'll keep the faith that goodness will come from our misfortune. I look at life and this new reality and how Ben's death has impacted everyone. I listen to each person's sadness, despair, and daily struggles going forward without Ben in our lives. Each person had their own relationship and their own experience of dealing with this new reality. Some people's instances are so raw and sad. Others are still in shock and despair, not only with their own loss, but with attempting to figure out how to support themselves and their loved ones as everyone moves forward. Ben's absence has left such a tremendous void in so many lives. People are seeking support from others while trying to support themselves. It's tremendous agony. It's so frustrating to explain the depth of sorrow we feel and face the reality that we must go forward in life.

One has to wonder and ask who truly is the victim of this new reality. The person who has taken their life is no longer enduring their pain in the *physical world, but those left behind remain in a position of uncertainty, muddling their way forward. It's mind-boggling. We're still here while our loved ones are hopefully in the position of peace that they desired. But it leaves us battling life, challenging us to make sense of something that is incomprehensible.*

The grief and void that we feel are undeniably the worst, most unbearable pain that one can feel. While others go about life in a way that we once knew, we only wish that we were in their position. Ben being here would make our lives "normal" again. I must accept that when we love someone so much, we must accept letting them go. It is their desire, even if it's not in our best interest and not something that we consented to. This reality is a huge thing to deal with.

2/12/2015

Received a text from Meghan this morning inviting me and Terry to a meeting at the Platteville Police Department. We're going to talk about presenting for the coordinated services team, which Meghan oversees through Grant County.

This is an outreach group for troubled youth and/or their family. A team will assess eligibility of the family and provide aid in resolving or assisting with challenges they face. Representatives from the state and other organizations in the community will be there. Meghan felt it would be good for us to partner with them to promote suicide prevention.

At noon, we met with Rick, the clinical social worker, and shared concerns about the girls. Rick encouraged us to urge both girls to seek out counseling to aid in expressing their feelings and their grief. One option is having them go to the mental health center of Dane County, a free service for those who don't have insurance. Unfortunately, we are in Grant County, so that would require a road trip from Platteville. He suggested we schedule time to talk as a family. He said that a mother is a family's emotional guide, while a dad is the reassuring and calm figure of the family. We left inspired and encouraged by Rick, as we always do. He's a very insightful, caring, faith-filled gentleman.

2/15/2015

I went into work, and Terry accompanied me. I knew it would be tough but didn't realize until I walked into my office just how tough it would be, especially looking around at all the pictures, mostly of kids. My office was just as it was the day I last worked. My, how things took a terrible turn, and look at where we are now ... without Benjamin. I looked through email communications with Ben prior to his death and sobbed reading them. He had such focus, determination, and motivation for future events and accomplishments. I had been very encouraged, and he seemed to be on the right track. We seemed to have regular communications. Such a good soul. There was nothing obvious in his emails that would suggest his suicide plan for Tuesday, November 11, 2014.

3/10/2016

I made it through another day at work without falling apart—until I got home. Neither Terry nor I slept well last night, and I was confident that the lack of sleep impacted our emotions. Our conversation led to us offending one another. We are both dealing with overwhelming emotions, and it seems the world is falling apart all around us. I went from running on the treadmill to showering and then going back to the bank to get my cell phone I'd left there. As I was returning home in Ben's car, I saw Terry at the intersection, heading away from our home. I came home and started to journal. After forty-five minutes, I called Terry to check on his whereabouts. He was at the storage unit we'd put Ben's items in. He came home, and shortly afterward, my sister, Pam, and her husband, Bruce, came over. Pam and I shared in conversation initially; later the guys joined us. Terry and I kissed goodnight and collapsed from exhaustion, praying for a new start and better day tomorrow.

6/14/2016

Yesterday, I shared with my boss that we have SOS Tuesday night and that Terry and I have a speaking engagement Wednesday with the Wisconsin Funeral Directors Association in Wisconsin Dells. She reassured me I can work on our speech at work, so I did. I want to convey to the attendees that Benjamin's death is not our first loss, so I am going to share with them the losses of our other young family members, including Greg, Chris, Tom, Laura, and Abby before disclosing Benjamin's death by suicide. This is obviously very emotional for me to do. In the midst of my writing, two coworker friends stopped by my office to talk with me.

My gut told me before they started speaking what the content of this conversation would be. Last year, our employee outing conflicted with the date of the first annual BENS Hope event. I attempted to be gracious about it last year, but was this going to happen again a year later? It was. As they spoke those words, I found myself reacting immediately with raw pain that flowed freely. My first words were, "Are you f'ing kidding me?!" There are 365 days in a year, and the only date that works for an employee outing is the same day as the second annual BENS Hope event? I was crushed, hurt, disappointed, and saddened that my friends would put me in this position again. As I tried to apologize for my reaction, they were also very aware of my pain as tears streamed down my face. I shared that the event we would be hosting was not like their event. The BENS Hope event was something I would rather not be hosting. I'd much rather have Benjamin here and alive. I excused myself and said I needed some air. I drove Ben's car home, crying all the way. Later, I walked back to work, still crying. People do not understand the depth of my pain nor do they have to. But I sure would have appreciated it if they had not put me in this position and had just gone with another date.

By the time I returned to work, an email had been sent to all employees about the employee event. I saw they selected a different date. Both of my friends who I talked to approached almost immediately upon my return, apologizing, which I appreciated. Now it was time to get back to the speech preparations.

Tonight, Tuesday night, was the SOS meeting. My emotional day flowed right into the evening at SOS. While typically I attempt to stay more composed, tonight I lost it a few times, but I allowed myself to be vulnerable in front of the attendees because this was how I was feeling. I realized we might all be here to work through our suicide recovery together, but that does not mean that we like it one bit.

6/12/2016

Terry and I spent days working on our presentation for the funeral directors' convention. With direction in my heart (placed there by God), we came up with an outline for our presentation. We wanted to share happy times ahead of the day that changed our lives forever. Terry suggested sharing some statistics. While the reality of suicide is incomprehensible, we wanted them to know that for every suicide there are twenty-five attempts! That means while Ben died by suicide, twenty-five others attempted to take their lives. When I look around at our SOS meetings, I contemplate this and the judgment that comes from our loss, but I'm also aware that others could be in our position. We will talk about the stigma of suicide, the role funeral directors play—how they can help and comfort families of suicide, the impact of their behaviors and actions— and close by providing information on our BENS Hope support group.

6/15/2016

I learned that Carrie was going to join us for today's travels to Wisconsin Dells for the presentation. Terry was elated about this, but I was having an array of emotions. How would Carrie feel about this as she attended? Would she be emotional, supportive, or would she critique us? I was not sure and came to the conclusion that God has this all figured out; He gave us the words, and now we just need to present it. I worked for half a day then came home to meet Carrie and Terry. I think everyone was a bit anxious, but we were together, and that is what mattered most. It was an enjoyable drive. We arrived forty-five minutes prior to our speaking engagement. Time for us to look over our speech and make notes. I was nervous and went to the bathroom at least four times before we spoke. As Carrie attached my microphone, I was clammy all over. These presentations are from our hearts and take so much for us emotionally, mentally, and physically to do. We know it is only by the grace of God that we are doing this!

Retelling Ben's story brings up very painful memories as we relive this experience, but we remind ourselves that if we can make the difference in one person's life, it is worth our time. We walked up on stage in front of the crowd and geared up the laptop behind us to display the BENS Hope website page. It was go time, and we did just that. After the initial first minutes of jitters calmed down, Terry and I took turns with our presentation. Carrie took pictures during this and also provided handouts and business cards to attendees. It felt like the presentation went exceptionally well, and the comments afterward validated our efforts. It was especially interesting to hear the host, Gary Woodka— who asked us to speak—as well as the participants say that they stayed to hear us. We get it, typically attendees skip out early on the last day of a conference, but they stayed to hear our story! And they shared the impact it had and various messages they took from it. We were told by attendees we should have been the keynote speakers. Wow! Terry, Carrie, and I gratefully accepted the accolades from those whom we visited with, and soon we got on the road and headed home. We stopped at the Sportspage Bar & Supper Club in Belmont for dinner to celebrate our accomplishment today.

6/29/2016

Two things came to mind on my morning bike ride, which I shared in a text I sent to Terry, Mandy, and Carrie. My first thought was that I need to start using the word "good" in greetings. I've used "morning" without "good" since Ben's suicide. Avoiding it suggests life isn't good, when it is. Why I decided to program my brain to think that the day cannot be "good" needs to stop today, and it is going to. So starting today, I will wish everyone a "Good Morning!" or a "Good Day!" I also decided to text family one thing daily to remind us that we are connected as we venture forth on our daily journey.

Today's one thing comes from Pastor Mark's sermon this past Sunday. I texted my family that whatever it is or was, whoever did or didn't do it, let it go. Might have to work to find our true, new happiness again, but I'm confident we can and will.

As the day transpired, an abundance of emails arrived with regard to the BENS Hope event. It's validation that this event is supposed to happen, which is very encouraging. I'm also overwhelmed to see that the *article submitted to the local paper regarding our speaking engagement at the Wisconsin Funeral Directors Convention ran in today's paper.*

I am encouraged to continue sharing our story in an effort to bring and offer suicide awareness and hope to the many others struggling. If we have the light from just a matchstick, it is still possible to bring light into the world of darkness. Thy will be done; not my will but God's.

Let your light so shine before men, that they may see your
good works, and glorify your Father which is in heaven.
Matthew 5:16 (KJV)

 8/1/2016: Carrie asked me to join her at 6 a.m. to start training for the second annual BENS Hope 5K run. As we were running and speaking of Ben, we looked down and there was a quarter. A Godwink that God and Ben are with us.

8/2/2016

The speaking engagement with the EMS crew at Southwest Health Center was this evening, and we invited some of our other SOS participants to share their stories. It was hard for them, but I was grateful they had the strength to share their stories in order to raise awareness and reduce the stigma of suicide. We speak of our children, spouses, siblings, family, and friends that we shared many wonderful moments with and lost to suicide. Their final act does not define them. Or us.

8/3/2016: It's Terry's birthday today. He texted to say he was having lunch with Ben. When I asked where he was, he said he was at the cemetery. Later, when Terry and I were in the car, my cell phone started to shut down. I picked it up only to see the different time zones displayed, which always reminds me of Ben since he worked with different areas in the country and knew the time zones. I reassured Terry this was a Godwink for his birthday.

8/6/2016

During my bike ride, I began thinking about how when suicide strikes your family, you now worry about what else will blindside you. While any death of a loved one leaves survivors devastated, suicide cannot be explained. You are suddenly expected to climb up the tallest mountain without any equipment. Thank goodness I had my faith and God who reached out His hand when I needed Him, which was constantly initially and often thereafter. I wanted to talk with some friends of mine who are mediums to ask if Ben's suicide was part of his journey. Then I realized, why not ask God? So I did. The reply I received was, "I knew you before you were in your mother's womb." The message is Ben's life, as all of ours, will play out as only God knows.

8/8/2016

Sometimes I feel like I'm trying to live two lives. One is my life working at the bank and the desire to give them the energy and attention needed to do my job. Then there's my brain occupied with thoughts of Ben's suicide, the stigma that comes with it, and my desire to speak out on this topic. Having endured many other losses of loved ones and knowing the support, love, and comfort I've received, I am painfully aware of the difference a death brings in people and their interactions—or lack of them—as with me and my family since Ben's suicide.

My urge to do something about this seems to take priority over the direction my life should be heading, thus changing the relevance in my daily work. I definitely appreciate my job at the bank and care for the people I work with, but I feel, and have felt since the night Ben took his life, that God has bigger things planned for me to do in this lifetime. I will continue to trust in Him and where life will take me. God has this journey planned out, not me. And whenever I think I have an idea or think I know what the day will bring, He lets me know otherwise. He's in charge.

With regard to BENS Hope, I received a call from Bennet, the reporter from the Telegraph Herald who asked to do a follow-up article on the one that ran a year ago on our efforts to raise suicide awareness. I asked my physician's assistant, Allison——who deals with depression, anxiety, bipolar disorder, and other mental health issues—to speak with him, and she agreed. I also asked my therapist, Candy, to share insights from her position as a professional who deals with those who are struggling as well as survivors of suicide. I am grateful for these two lovely ladies for sharing their perspectives.

8/13/2016

Saturday morning. I woke up and asked God what He had in mind for me today. I knew I needed to go to work for a couple hours, and I had promised to spend time with Judy, a retired coworker. Terry wanted to deliver BENS Hope posters, and I wanted to get in some exercise. Wasn't sure how everything would fit in. Trusted God had it all figured out. I was guided to walk to work, spent a couple hours there, then walked home. I put on my BENS Hope T-shirt, and Terry and I headed out the door.

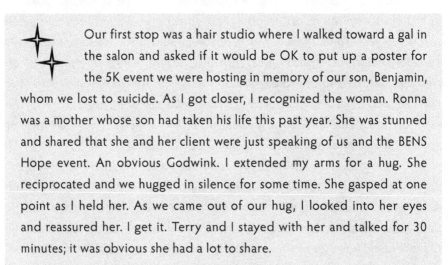

Our first stop was a hair studio where I walked toward a gal in the salon and asked if it would be OK to put up a poster for the 5K event we were hosting in memory of our son, Benjamin, whom we lost to suicide. As I got closer, I recognized the woman. Ronna was a mother whose son had taken his life this past year. She was stunned and shared that she and her client were just speaking of us and the BENS Hope event. An obvious Godwink. I extended my arms for a hug. She reciprocated and we hugged in silence for some time. She gasped at one point as I held her. As we came out of our hug, I looked into her eyes and reassured her. I get it. Terry and I stayed with her and talked for 30 minutes; it was obvious she had a lot to share.

We walked down Main Street and entered a store. A mailman Terry had once worked with came into the same store, and we showed him our posters. The mailman told us of his brother's suicide. He was the first one to arrive at the scene after receiving a call from his sister-in-law. Listening to him, we learned he struggled with how some of the officials handled the suicide when they arrived. We knew it was no coincidence that we ran into him because in the future, we would be going to the police department to make presentations, and he had important insight to share.

8/18/2016

During our second presentation at the police department, the mailman, John, joined us along with other SOS participants who took the stage to present their stories. John was the last one up. He first commented that he knew hats were not allowed, but he was wearing one that was his brother Bill's: the guy he admired and looked up to his entire life, the guy he found dead by suicide.

John was gracious and honest about the evening of his brother's death. He shared how he had called and gave the address where there had been the shooting. He stated his brother had killed himself and was deceased. The 911 dispatcher asked urgently for the closest intersection to the home. John questioned this since he had given the specific address. As he listened to sirens around town and awaited the officials, an EMT was the first to respond. She was kind and asked to see Bill, just to ensure there was nothing more she could do to help him. John waited outside, waving his arms as he noticed police. He stated it was like a SWAT team coming in. There was apparently a misunderstanding of the "shooting." The officer in charge was loud and condescending. He was yelling at the EMT, telling her to get out of the house. As if the suicide wasn't horrible enough for John's brother's widow, now they stood listening to the officer reprimanding the EMT. He painted a not-so-pretty picture of the police, but it was important for John to share with the officials what not to do at the scene of a suicide.

11/8/2016

We had SOS with thirteen in attendance. We had two teenagers, a young boy and a young girl, who attended with their mom. Both teens were familiar with and experienced losses to suicide. During the meeting, they shared that they had hosted a haunted house on a family farm and raised money that they wished to donate to BENS Hope to help. We asked how the money could best help. One of their ideas was to offer it as a scholarship. We were astonished at their efforts and desire to help when most avoid the topic of suicide. They continued their conversation, asking if BENS Hope could help their friends who thought suicide was the answer to their problems! Our mouths dropped and stomachs turned. These kids are sixth graders! Lord, please protect the children in our world and let our story offer them insight.

11/11/2016

The days leading up to the anniversary of Ben's suicide were intense, and it seemed that Terry, Mandy, Carrie, and I each had endured complete meltdowns on different days. It helped to be there to support each other. But as a mom, it was difficult knowing my family was hurting and there was no way for me to take away this pain.

God has told me several times that we are on a sole journey. I have learned this to be so true. I believe each of us have our own "sole" journey that will transform our "soul" during our time on this earth in preparation for what's ahead. And the interesting part is that while we can support each other, we cannot walk another's journey for them. I pray that we can offer support to each other; the pain and anguish that come from grieving will be felt by each of us differently and at different times based on the circumstances around us.

On this day of this year, Terry and I had scheduled our first ninety-minute stone massage appointments. Not surprisingly, when I reached out to schedule the massages, out of all the dates we would be in the area, the only date open for the massage therapy was on November 11, 2016. A definite Godwink for us. We believe Ben wanted us to find relief and relaxation on the second anniversary of his passing. We believe signs like this (however they work) from Ben, God, or Spirit are the Godwinks we need to propel us forward on our journey.

CHAPTER 7

WITNESSING A SUICIDAL CRISIS FIRSTHAND

Fear not, for I am with you; be not dismayed, for I am your God;
I will strengthen you, I will help you, I will uphold
you with my righteous right hand.
Isaiah 41:10 (ESV)

While you may or may not have an appreciation for the story I'm about to share, as you read on, you will understand how it is relevant. Previously, I didn't understand what, if anything, could be done to help someone who is suicidal. But as God would have it, He brought me into a situation where I would not only witness a person in crisis but also be involved in their survival. Please note that this story may be triggering.

11/13/2016

Upon our return home from Door County, Carrie texted me. She asked that I read a post from my sister-in-law, Jenny, but added to be prepared. The post was about Jenny's child who had been rushed to the American Family Children's Hospital in Madison. She was very sick, dehydrated, and had flatlined at one point on November 11. The little girl was revived and put on a ventilator. In the Facebook post, Jenny asked, "Please pray that God would restore her health, that there would be no long-term damage, physically or cognitively, and that she would be able to come home soon. Please pray also for God's peace and comfort for our family and for us to get some much-needed rest. We know God is sovereign. Thank you all so much."

In the days that followed, Jenny and her husband, Kurt, worked to manage their four kids at home with some normalcy while knowing the seriousness of this situation as their child remained in the ICU at the hospital in Madison. At some point during all of this, Jenny and Kurt requested assistance from their family, friends, and church family. With Kurt having to return to work December 1, additional help was needed. I admired their courage for reaching out and asking for help.

We're accustomed to quick, short responses from people when they are asked, "How are you today?" They usually say OK, fine, or good. These are common responses said in passing; however, if we all answered with authentic responses, we might say we're feeling tired, sad, lonely, overwhelmed, stressed, exhausted, depleted, or worried about a loved one. Please know it's OK not to be OK.

12/4/2016

We were hit with a winter storm. What can we expect? It's Wisconsin in December. This is not a problem if you are able to stay put, but traveling this day was a must. Today, Mandy would celebrate her graduation from culinary school in Milwaukee. Not only was it graduation, but the culinary graduates were also preparing a five-course dinner for the guests they invited. As Terry and I listened, Mandy's conversation got tearful and broken up with moments of silence as she tried to compose herself. She shared the nightmare her travels had been so far and her concerns for our safety traveling to Milwaukee. We reassured Mandy we would be there to support and cheer her on as we always have been.

It was a white-knuckle ride to Milwaukee, and considering we saw cars in the ditch every five minutes, we had to ask ourselves if we had made the best decision. Needless to say, it was a long ride there, but thank God we arrived safely and enjoyed a wonderful evening watching Mandy in the food line prepping food. We enjoyed a delicious dinner. Chef came out to announce the students after we finished our meals. The look on Mandy's face validated that she is doing what she loves, and we were witness to that, which was priceless! Our travels back to Madison were less intense, but I must admit we were very grateful once we got back to Mandy and Brian's and snuggled into our PJs.

12/5/2016

The next morning, we decided to take a stroll to the coffee shop where we chatted about a family vacation over Ben's would-be thirtieth birthday. We considered California. Ben had traveled there for work and loved it so much he thought he might stay. Reflecting on those words seemed to bring comfort knowing that our family trip would include Ben somehow, some way.

I noticed that I had a missed call from my sister-in-law, Jenny, who'd been struggling with her child's health situation. After we got back to Mandy's place, I stepped into the bedroom to return Jenny's call. As I talked with her, it was apparent she was struggling. I listened and asked questions, but I was not prepared to hear what she shared: "I'm not doing well. I cannot deal with everything going on. This is too much!" As I reassured Jenny that things would get better, she dropped the bomb: "I was going to take my life Saturday night. I was in the kitchen pantry and wanted to end all of this." I could not breathe or believe I was hearing this from Jenny, a mother with wonderful children, living in a beautiful home she and her loving and devoted husband had built. They, like Terry and I, were church-going people, and Jenny was a faith-filled woman. Was she really saying these words to me? I remained calm, possibly due to the shock I was in, but reassured Jenny we would get her the help she needed. Jenny told me she had called five offices that morning requesting to see someone who could help her, and only one of the five facilities offered to see her. I was shocked and wondered what others do when they are in crisis if the resources nearby lack the immediate opportunity to give the support needed.

I offered Jenny my counseling appointment that was scheduled the following day and reassured her that Candy, my counselor, would help her. I then gave my family an update on Jenny immediately afterwards. They were all shocked. Carrie, who holds a psychology degree, inquired if I'd asked Jenny how she intended to take her life. That was a piece of information I neglected to ask, so when I called Jenny back a few minutes later, I did ask her that specific question. Ask, do they have a plan? If so, do not leave them, remove harmful items, call 911. Jenny was just leaving her house to head to the appointment at the clinic that offered to see her. We talked as she drove into town. As we did, I inquired how she intended to take her life. An overdose. She was going to take pills. I was still in disbelief but heard her loud and clear. I texted Jenny the National Suicide Prevention Helpline number, 1-800-273-8255, and the TEXT HOPELINE number, 741741, as additional resources with immediate help available. During our phone conversation, Jenny seemed to be doing better. She had a new focus and was hopeful that the clinic visit would help her. It was also encouraging to know she had the option to see my counselor the following day.

We had gotten her over the hump for now. As she arrived at the clinic for her appointment, I reassured her I would check in again later, and I did. What she shared was disheartening. The clinician was no help at all, and after only a few minutes in, Jenny knew it was a waste of time. After twelve minutes, she left! I was sickened to think a person having suicidal thoughts was left to walk out a door by a clinician! The experience at the clinic left us all shocked and disappointed. Fortunately, when Jenny left the clinic, she went to see Meghan Skemp, a former social worker and current colleague. This is the exact person who came to my mind for Jenny to meet up with.

I texted Jenny at 7:18 p.m. She said meeting with Meghan was helpful, and she was feeling better. As I headed to bed around 9 p.m., I texted Jenny, wishing her a good night of sleep and reassured her she would enjoy meeting Candy the following day.

12/6/2016

It was around 5:45 a.m. the following morning when I got an urgent

*God nudge to stop by Jenny's home. I got up, showered, and got ready
for work. Terry was cleaning snow off of Ben's car when I got a text from
Jenny at 6:17 a.m. Jenny asked if I was still able to come over and help
with the kids, which I had offered the day prior to do. I told her I was
already on my way. Little did I know how the day would play out.*

*When I arrived, Jenny was lying on the kitchen floor in a fetal position.
It was apparent that she had not yet showered nor did it look like she
had gotten any sleep or eaten. For the sake of the kids, I asked Jenny
if she would like to return to her bed upstairs or go to the sofa in their
family room, off of the kitchen floor and out of direct view of her kids.
Jenny declined, so I worked around her and assisted the kids as they got
breakfast and prepared their lunches for school.*

*Shortly after, my sister-in-law, Betty—Jenny's sister—arrived. She
had stopped by on her way to work to check in. As she did, she visited
with the kids, encouraging them for their day ahead. Betty helped the
kids to the school bus. Jenny used what little energy she had to make
her way to the kids, offering them hugs and well-wishes for their day.
Once Jenny's children and sister left, I figured I had a few more minutes
to spend with Jenny before heading to work. However, over the next few
minutes, it became very apparent I would not be going into work as I
watched Jenny spiral from being overwhelmed to becoming suicidal right
before my very eyes.*

*Jenny sat in front of me on the floor with her knees pulled up and
her arms wrapped around them, rocking feverishly. She shared that
she had lost fifteen pounds in the past three weeks. It was apparent she
was anxious as she ran her hands over her arms and along her body to
her feet and then back again repeatedly. I knew not having slept, eaten,
or showered contributed to her condition. As I observed her, I noticed
her pupils were extremely small, and when she talked with me, she was
looking at me, but I didn't feel she could actually see me. I spoke gently
to Jenny, reassuring her that she would get through this. But it was
apparent Jenny had momentarily lost all faith. She repeated through her
tears that she just could not do this any longer. I knew there was no
possible way Jenny could be left alone today. It was within a short time*

that I texted my boss at work, explaining that I was concerned Jenny may harm herself if left unattended, and therefore, I would not make it into work today. As we talked, Jenny continued to spiral, often running to a bucket she had nearby, dry heaving. She kept saying she could not get sick and that she needed to keep her medicine down. Knowing she had just started on medication, I asked for her doctor's name, and she felt we should call him. I also asked Jenny if I should take her to a hospital. She answered without certainty. One of her children had a concert Friday night, and she did not want to be away for that. I called her doctor's office and was connected with the triage nurse. Explaining the situation, the nurse asked that I not leave Jenny alone. I reassured her that I would not and that I had lost my son, Ben, to suicide. I knew it was not in our best interest to leave Jenny alone.

A few minutes later, her doctor called back to speak with me. He stated that the medication prescribed to Jenny was to help her reduce stress and aid in getting sleep. It could take one to three weeks to fully get into her system. Also, a side effect of stopping abruptly was suicidal thoughts. When I inquired about admitting Jenny to a hospital, he said I should take her to Madison if it came to that. I shared this conversation with Jenny. At times she seemed to understand, while other times it seemed she could not process anything I was saying. Her own world was consumed by darkness and despair. While the experience was overwhelming for me, it was also eye-opening knowing that I was right there offering support and hope yet she could not hear or see what I was saying.

This proved true as I showed her pictures on the wall of her family—pictures of her and Kurt, pictures of each of the kids—and I explained to her how badly her family needed her in their lives. She stood next to me listening, only to fall to the floor again and start rocking back and forth, repeating that she could not do this. She could not handle what God had presented to her nor did she see any hope in the matter. She could only hear Satan whispering lies about the future. It was sad to witness how this beautiful, faith-filled person had lost all hope. I reminded her of our loving God and that through Him all things are possible. I reassured Jenny that because of our loving God, I was still on this earth. It was because of my faith that even through the darkness and sadness of all the losses we've endured and, most recently, Ben's suicide, God is here to pick us up every time we fall.

As I was writing *Tears of Love* and reviewing this section of the journal entries, I found myself reflecting on a beautiful poem I recited daily called "Footprints in the Sand." It honestly helped me profusely through my struggles, and I pray it offers comfort to any of you struggling as well.

Footprints in the Sand

One night I dreamed I was walking along the beach with the Lord.

Many scenes from my life flashed across the sky.

In each scene, I noticed footprints in the sand.

Sometimes there were two sets of footprints, other times there was one set of footprints.

This bothered me because I noticed that during the low periods of my life, when I was suffering from anguish, sorrow, or defeat, I could see only one set of footprints.

So I said to the Lord, "You promised me, Lord, that if I followed you, you would walk with me always.

But I have noticed that during the most trying periods of my life there have only been one set of footprints in the sand. Why when I needed you most have you not been there for me?"

The Lord replied, "The times when you have seen only one set of footprints in the sand is when I carried you."

Friends, I share with you that as I just typed this poem, I was overcome with emotion. I wept. Maybe you can relate or maybe not. Regardless, this poem has power and saved me countless times. I honestly did not have the capacity on many occasions following Ben's suicide to do much except breathe, and that took everything I had in me. I did not think it was possible to go on. Quite honestly, I did not know if I wanted to. But by the grace of God, by the blessing of this poem, I am here, and I am thankful to know that God does carry us through the times we don't have the ability to make it on our own. If you don't feel you have the capacity to go on, I encourage you to seek God, who will carry you. And now back to my day with Jenny.

As I took Jenny and sat her on the sofa next to me, she asked me how I was able to find the strength to get through life as it has presented itself to me. I reassured her it was my faith. I explained to her that I know what it is like to get through one minute at a time, one hour at a time. It's just taking it slow and keeping the faith that you can deal with whatever life presents to you. It doesn't mean you like what has been presented or want what has been presented, but it's to keep the faith that you can do it!

I asked her what we could do to release some of the stress and burden that she was feeling. She said going to the hospital overwhelmed her. She could not handle going there. There was a constant source of anxiety when she was there, and she felt shame as she admitted this, but it was the truth. (We would later learn that Jenny was dealing with post-traumatic stress disorder.) I reassured Jenny that if this was causing her such strife, then she did not have to do this right now. If this was too much for her to handle, then she could give it up to God. She looked at me and said, "Really?" She had not considered this as an option. Once she realized this, she felt immediate relief, and I could see it wash over her.

I encouraged Jenny to eat, which she declined to do. But she did agree to grab a shower. As she went upstairs, I tidied up around the house, which was in a state of disarray—very unusual for the Jenny I knew. It validated that the Jenny we loved was struggling. Fortunately, her toddler son, Keegan, kept entertained between watching TV, eating saltine crackers—making a mess of them everywhere—and playing on the iPad. I thank Jesus that Keegan was preoccupied and not aware of the severity of his mother's condition.

As elated as I was that Jenny agreed to shower, I walked upstairs several times to ensure she was OK. As she came out from the bathroom wrapped in a towel, it was apparent that exhaustion overcame her as she retreated to the bedroom floor. We continued to talk for some time. I continued to offer her support and encouragement. After a while, she reassured me she was OK and would finish getting ready and meet me downstairs.

When she came downstairs, her transformation was apparent!

This brings to mind something I wish to share with you. We cannot tell what a person is feeling internally based on what they portray externally. I've heard on multiple occasions how pretty or handsome someone was, gifted or talented, outgoing or friendly, happy or kind. Again, don't let someone's exterior deter you from asking about how their interior is feeling. It could be lifesaving.

As I prepared some toast for Jenny to eat, she called her friend, Chelsea, to see if she could watch Keegan. When Chelsea arrived, we sat and visited for quite some time until Chelsea left with Keegan. Upon their departure, Jenny and I headed into town for Jenny's first counseling appointment with Candy. Jenny asked if I would come into her counseling session with her, so of course I said yes. Upon our arrival at the office, Candy met us in the waiting room and greeted me with her usual hug. Jenny looked at me immediately, smiled, and said, "I like her already." Over the course of the next hour, Candy and I witnessed through Jenny's tears the emotional roller coaster she was riding on. As draining as it was for Jenny to share and for us to hear, I'm confident that she left with a much-needed sense of hope. We all need hope! Candy released Jenny into my care, but only if I promised to have her in constant care over the course of the next seventy-two hours, which I agreed to.

When we got home, the next point of business was getting Jenny some real food to eat. She finally did eat! The stress had lifted; she felt hope and found her appetite! We turned on Family Life Radio to celebrate and even lit a candle on the counter. Won't the kids be surprised to walk in and see this vision of their mother versus the environment they had left earlier that morning. It was the breath of fresh air that everyone needed. We then realized we needed to call Kurt and prepare him with what had transpired over the course of the day. Jenny asked if I would call and talk to Kurt, so I did. I shared everything, even Candy's comment that Jenny needs to focus on herself because if she doesn't take care of herself right now, she won't be here to take care of anyone later. I can only imagine the bomb Kurt must have felt we dropped on him. When Kurt got home, we talked some more. Shortly afterward, the kids got home from school. It was a very joyful reunion.

Terry came and joined us for dinner that evening. Our prayers were ones of hope and faith for everyone. It was apparent as we were saying our goodbyes that Kurt was still trying to process all of this. Completely understandable. I felt the reality of the day hit me as I drove home. I reflected on the hugs and thank yous and praised God. I knew very well that the outcome of this day could have been very different and that this family could have been planning a funeral.

I realize this is an extremely intense situation, but I think it's important for you to hear about it because it's a part of my journey that God apparently wanted me to witness. While I had no idea what this day would bring, God gave me strength and self-control, which allowed me to remain calm and courteous when, in essence and in these circumstances, I could have gone berserk. It was another great challenge that God saw me through and obviously was a matter of life and death. As dire of a situation this was, my prayers for those of you reading are that this story will offer you or your loved one struggling some insight and that you will realize there is hope that you can go on.

Seek help; it's available. While it's common to hold others accountable for our circumstances in life, good or bad, we are responsible. So for those of you who wish to have a leading role, you do! It's your very own unique life story! While we obviously aren't in control of all that happens to us, we are responsible for how we react to it and move forward in it.

Following Ben's death, I had a dream relevant to where my life was at the time. Two options were put in front of me, I believe, and they were pertinent to my decision to stay in this world. I dreamed that I had just parked my vehicle at what appeared to be a drive-in movie theater. As I exited the driver's side, I realized I had just stepped into quicksand and immediately began sinking. I looked around, witnessing people in all directions, and while it was my instinct to cry out for help, I didn't. I found myself contemplating what to do and thinking of Benjamin as my body sank deeper and deeper. I had two options. I could choose to succumb to my circumstances or remain in this world. It was my choice! Nobody else's.

Regardless of what others do or how they make us feel, we are responsible for ourselves and the decisions we make in our circumstances. I thought of Benjamin and how in a moment, if I elected to, all the pain in losing him would be over. And then my thoughts went to Terry, Mandy, Carrie, my mom, and my sister, knowing very well the extreme pain this aftermath would cause them. How could I put them through that again? Soon the quicksand touched my chin before reaching my clenched mouth and finally making its way beneath my nostrils. This crucial decision awaited my action. Time was running out! And in the next moment, I found myself tilting my head backwards with my nostrils upward and was saved.

I believe God used this demonstration to help me understand these choices are ours to make. He gave me the option to stay or go on, and staying here means doing the work He chose and telling Ben's story, our story, over and over again to help others. Let me reassure you, it is not easy. And as jarring as the day with Jenny was, I believe God wanted me there to witness firsthand the despair and darkness she was living in. Even being with Jenny in person, highlighting all her blessings in life, she could not comprehend what I was saying. She was deep in the well of darkness, a place I knew well and had been in myself. It's a place that encases and impacts you mentally, physically, spiritually, and emotionally, whispering all sorts of lies. Sometimes the darkness causes such despair that the light cannot be seen, and this was an example of that firsthand.

Maybe this was insight on how Ben felt? And as horrific as it was to experience, it served a purpose and became part of this book. Why?

To offer hope to those in darkness. It's these hardships that make us stronger, even though it may not feel like it as we experience them. It is on my heart to encourage and remind you that no matter how bad things get in life, you can survive. I am living proof of this. I contemplated checking out on multiple occasions and know what it feels like to be in the clutches of darkness, hanging on by a thread, literally clinging by my fingertips in a well so deep, but God kept me here to be a light and offer you hope. Do I have it all figured out? Heck no! I'm still learning every day, just like you are, through hardships and blessings. But when I am presented with opportunities to support others, whatever they may be, the warmth that fills my soul is hard to describe. I imagine that's because my new mission in life comes from God, and my identity holds a new and powerful purpose helping others. What do you say? Are you in? Let's do this thing called life! I'm here for you, flawed but authentic. And now back to my journal entries.

12/29/2016

During Bible study, I asked my brother-in-law, Ken, what happens to us when we die. Ken shared that we become a spiritual being. I asked him, "Where do we go?" He answered, "Heaven." I asked him where heaven is. Is it right here, up there, or where does heaven reside? I know it is a mystery and for none of us to completely understand, but I do believe with all my heart in God and in His son, Jesus, and that in death we are born again and reunited with those we've loved and who have died and gone before us. And one day, what a reunion it will be!

Interestingly enough, during my morning prayers over the next week or so, I asked God to help me make sense of all this. I was reassured that we all walk together. I was told that our deceased ones are walking alongside us in spirit and that their presence is as real as our living loved ones walking with us. Wow! This brought me a sense of joy.

✝ **1/3/2017:** Over the week, a few things occurred that I didn't initially think much of until the third incident. Then I put things together, which seemed to validate this thought that our deceased loved ones are still walking with us. The first incident occurred while I was sitting in my office. I heard a commotion that I assumed was coming from outside of the building, so I immediately dismissed it. It wasn't until I left my office and returned when I noticed Ben's framed picture on my fireproof file cabinet had fallen. Ben's picture was facing up, and the glass was intact. It appeared the matting on the frame was no longer adhered to the frame itself. I made a note to take this home and have Terry repair it, then went on with my day.

The second incident occurred Friday, January 6, 2017. I had gotten home earlier in the day, and after trying to log on to the internet without success, I ended up cleaning out our kitchen cabinets. Three boxes later, Terry came home. He assisted me in getting logged into the computer. I had talked with my boss on how I'm now enjoying using comp time to work on BENS Hope initiatives. Devoting my time to the American Foundation of Suicide Prevention (AFSP), BENS Hope, and other initiatives has become a priority. Using comp time to do this while still fulfilling work duties has brought peace and comfort to my heart and mind. As I worked on composing a letter to AFSP, I continued to spill my heart out. Around 9:30 p.m., after I emailed this letter, I started to type an email to friends Matt and Meghan, reflecting on the holidays and recent death of Matt's dad, Leo. As I typed away, it was at the moment I was reassuring them that I was confident Leo and Ben had celebrated Christmas together in heaven when I sensed someone to my left. I was positive I felt someone or an energy there, so I turned my head in that direction; it was as though someone slipped from my sight. Suddenly, I was filled with a power surge that shot throughout my entire body and literally took my breath away; I softly called out, "God? Jesus? Ben?" I was not sure who was with me, but I was absolutely certain I had a visitor. I believe this was a gift God had given to me. The experience startled me, but I was not afraid.

Within five minutes, Terry walked in the door. As I shared this with him, I wept. It was an amazing feeling of love and disbelief of the power and comfort this experience had brought and left me with. The following morning, as Terry went into the garage to move Ben's car out, I heard a familiar noise that reminded me of the day Ben's picture frame fell down in my office. As I ran to the entryway and peeked out into the garage, I asked Terry what the noise was. He replied that as he backed out of the garage, the door came down on Ben's car then bounced back up. It's not the fact that these instances happened, it's the timing of when they happened. After a recent conversation at Bible study, I now pray about our loved ones in spirit. Just because we can't see them does not mean they are not here.

1/29/2017

I just sent an email to SOS friends Pam and Dennis, who lost their son Tanner to suicide in 2014. It is her birthday and Tanner's birthday in heaven. They offer an SOS support group in La Crosse. They were a Godsend to us and offered hope that both our families would get through the loss of our sons to suicide. Thank you, Dennis and Pam! You are a blessing to us and truly a gift and light to so many.

1/30/2017

The past two weeks have been full of struggle—mentally, physically, and emotionally—not only for me but for my family. Typically, it seems when one of us is down the others are there to cheer us on. Lately it seems everyone is having their struggles at the same time. I want to be their cheerleader, but it takes all I can just to be my own cheerleader. In addition to the Wisconsin winters' snow, ice, and sleet, the sun is nowhere to be seen. Winter is day after day of grayness, which serves as a big, frigid blanket of depression.

Everyone seems to be taking their turns with a cold, the flu, or both. I've had this feeling before—you are on a hamster wheel, running in circles but getting nowhere. It is a helpless feeling and you have to ask, "How long can this go on?" Going through the motions in life without feeling gratitude for anything is quite frustrating. You know it's going to be a long day when you wake up tired. Regardless of this condition, I force myself to get on the treadmill, even if only for one mile. Fortunately, I usually make it a few miles and am thankful when I do. I've never regretted exercising! As I head to work, I pray, reminding myself of others who are struggling and reflecting on the many blessings I sometimes can't see. Getting through the day has been another challenge when I'm feeling like I haven't gotten enough sleep the night prior. As I work my way through the day, I am elated when it's time to come home, yet only get into my PJs, eat, and realize that in a few short hours, this cycle will repeat itself once again.

2/6/2017

Terry and I had a meeting with UW-Platteville campus police to share our story and also discuss the number of students they encounter on a regular basis who are struggling or in crisis. We offered them BENS Hope brochures and asked that they share them with any students they encounter to let them know there is hope for them and that SOS will be expanding to the UW-P campus to offer them support. Interesting how the lead cop, Joe, had encountered a number of suicides in his career, but it was obvious none had touched him personally. How fortunate for him. He was definitely a "head thinker" as he shared with us. The other officers were "heart thinkers," and it was apparent that either suicide had touched them in their lives or our personal story had. We thanked God for this meeting and the opportunity to raise awareness and extend support to others who are struggling.

2/7/2017

I had a long awaited, much-needed appointment with Candy tonight. I cried the first half hour of counseling, but I guess it needed to happen. I told her I'd seen a post on Facebook that Terry's sister had posted. She was wishing her son, Anthony, a happy thirtieth. Anthony was one month older to the day than Benjamin. She acknowledged what a blessing Anthony was and how proud she was of his accomplishments, as a proud mom would and should do. As I read the post, I found myself overwhelmed with despair, not because of what was said but because of the reality of what we would not be able to experience. We would not be able to celebrate with Ben or enjoy his upcoming thirtieth birthday. We would not celebrate his engagement or wedding, or, for me, the mother-son dance. All these celebrations were canceled when Ben took his life, and the reality of that played over and over in my heart and mind as I read through posts and conversations of others who eagerly share their loved one's experiences.

This is by no means to take away from others; it is just difficult for me to process. I cry my tears of love, knowing what our family looked so forward to with Ben will never be a reality.

I also caught up with Jenny and Kurt. It's been a couple of months since that dreary December day when Jenny was contemplating taking her life. I am so thankful for listening to that God nudge I received on December 6. I recall the scene I witnessed as I arrived that morning and the trauma as the day played out. I am thankful to God for saving Jenny and giving their family the strength and support to get through that together. My heart aches knowing that our story of Ben's suicide and the emptiness my family feels will remain the same. He is dead and will not be coming home, ever. I pray each and every day for God to continue to walk with me and our family and to heal our hearts and help us find goodness in this tragedy.

2/8/2017

Terry and I met with people at Clarity Clinic. We reviewed and discussed the program they developed to aid in suicide prevention efforts as we go into the schools. Our perspectives differed. They based their approach on their teaching intentions; we based ours on our experience. We want to make the most of our time with these students and make the biggest impact possible so they realize that suicide should never be an option and that suicide is truly a permanent solution to a temporary situation.

2/9/2017

Had our first SOS at UW-Platteville's campus. Bless the campus counselor, Jason's, heart for agreeing to start this group, but apparently there needs to be improvements with advertising efforts. The only attendees were the three students who came to our other SOS group. The good news is that Jason saw the interaction between us and the students. There's an organic relationship we've developed: one of care, trust, and even love. If the students came to SOS in despair and feeling misunderstood, they left feeling they could smile again. It was good for Terry and me to also see this transformation. God is good, and we are witnessing blessings right before our eyes.

2/12/2017

We invited Josh, a student from UW-P who attended the SOS group, to join us at church. We were confident he'd feel the love we have gotten so accustomed to. Love my church! We are keeping the faith that one day our family may offer hope and light to others in darkness.

2/13/2017

Woke up a few times during the night to go to the bathroom then started feeling anxiety in the early morning. Couldn't understand why then realized it was the feeling I had to go into work and put on a brave face and fake smile to ensure everyone felt good when they offered me birthday wishes. I was so overwhelmed I felt sick to my stomach. I just don't have the energy to fake my way through today. I am hurting and missing Ben. I feel like I can't breathe, so much so that I feel like I'm sinking in quicksand again and can't come up for air, and tears fall like a stream of constant flowing water. After I texted work informing them I would not be coming in, I fell back into bed and fell asleep. It was 9:20 when I awoke. I still felt sad but somewhat rested. I wept most of the morning; it's how I get through life now. I allow myself to cry when I need to, which I think can heal my broken heart. There are many tears because there is so much love for Ben and my family. I asked Terry if we could drop our taxes off, a goal I try to accomplish each year by my birthday.

We stop first, though, at Erschen's Florists to purchase a single rose. Then it's off to the cemetery. I don't often make it a point to go there, but today I feel the need to go, so we do. At the cemetery, the floodgates open once again. My heart aches as I place the rose at Ben's gravesite. I take Terry's hands and ask if we can pray The Lord's Prayer. My birthday was a day when I always heard from Ben; he never missed my special day. This new reality of not hearing from him is something that breaks my heart. I am confident of the other signs validating that our loved ones are still with us, but it's not the same. We ended the day at a favorite restaurant in Madison, saying a prayer of thanks for our day and blessings. I looked into Terry's eyes and expressed my thanks for his support today. He reciprocated. I love him so much, and there is no one I can imagine being with besides him to walk and fall with on this journey.

2/14/2017

Valentine's Day! We hosted SOS that evening. Terry and I decided to treat attendees to pizza for dinner. No newbies showed up, but most of the regulars did. Worked out nicely, and I was able to share the hardships of the week with my birthday and missing Ben. Other attendees also had hardships they shared with upcoming anniversaries. One lost her husband to suicide by gunshot, coming up on five years ago; another lost her sibling one year ago. We are thankful for the blessing that SOS is and all the wonderful and courageous people we have crossed paths with on our journey.

2/17/2017

Terry and I made a trip to visit with two of our favorite people, Sister Kay and Sister Marie, who invited us to church and dinner. Sister Kay was busy getting ready for their upcoming jubilee, so we spent time with Sister Marie, who, at eighty-four years old, is quite the lady! She enjoyed showing us her paintings and craft room. Such talent! Sister Kay was able to join us by dinnertime. These women loved introducing us to others and sharing our ministry of helping others touched by suicide. We feel like it's show-and-tell when we visit. We stayed and talked for a few hours. Time went by quickly. In addition to the many topics covered, we also discussed hearing God, which not all people understand. We were encouraged to keep doing what God has chosen as our ministry in life, so that is what we plan to do. And with the help from others whom God places in our path, we trust His plan with all our hearts.

2/21/2017

Terry and I attended a meeting hosted by the Lafayette County Rural Safety Coalition. We were not sure what to expect at this meeting, so we took BENS Hope brochures and our business cards. Little did we know we would be given the floor and asked to share our story of Ben and the intentions of BENS Hope. This is never easy, and we never get through it without getting emotional. While BENS Hope started out with the intent to offer support to other suicide survivors, we've since learned of the stigma associated with suicide deaths, which also follows people who have attempted suicide. As others learn of it, people who are already struggling are then treated differently as the stigma sets in. Our message is to remind those contemplating suicide of the grief they will inflict on those left behind. As excruciating as these stories are to us, our reality does make an impact on others.

Carrie made a profound statement with regard to these concerns, saying, "Mom, we should not try to scream our story to people who will never get it but whisper it to those who do." Wow! Amen to this statement. Thank you for insight and sharing with me, Carrie! So true.

My evening wrapped up with a counseling appointment with Candy, who reminded me that in addition to helping others, it is important to take care of myself. I asked her for input on our plans to attend an upcoming suicide coalition event. I knew a lot of mental health professionals would attend. I wondered if she felt they would learn anything from us. I was moved with her response when she shared, "Of all the education I've had, I've learned the most from your experience following Ben's suicide." Little did we realize the number of people, or in which ways, that Ben's suicide has and will continue to make an impact on. We are reminded of the promise we heard from God the night of Ben's suicide. You will find *goodness in this. And comments like hers validate God's promise.*

4/6/2017

Today, Terry and I have a presentation at UW-Platteville. Preparing for this week has been extremely difficult. I want to make our Heavenly Father proud, but I also want to ensure that our message reaches into the hearts of all those attending. Our goal is to offer hope and to encourage others to open the door and let Jesus in. I explained this to Terry, as I was feeling overwhelmed and really needed his input with the presentation efforts. I realized this was hard for Terry as well. He is Ben's dad and lost his son, his only son, to suicide. Terry is an introvert and an empath like Benjamin. I admire Terry profusely for putting his love for Benjamin ahead of his fear of speaking in front of an audience to honor Ben and serve God in the capacity He has chosen for us.

Terry and I worked on the presentation in the evenings twice this week to prepare. I was pleased when Terry offered content to aid in presentation ideas. He had chosen the cord of three strands passage from scripture to read and an email he received from our friend, Sister Kay. Sister Kay acknowledged our spiritual journey of growth and how Ben lives on through us as we all change lives through BENS Hope. Not sure how many times I revised our script; I only know that God guided both our thoughts and words.

Terry had the car packed with BENS Hope items. Terry and I finally took our items on stage and noticed the room was set up for around 250 attendees. Mom manned the BENS Hope table as usual, distributing items and explaining our mission. She's such an advocate for us and BENS Hope; we are so thankful and blessed. When we took the stage, it was the first time my heart raced at this level. I was so nervous! Thankfully, Terry started our presentation, and within seconds, it was apparent God was with us. Terry spoke confidently, interjecting comments that filled the room with laughter. His ease immediately brought me calm. As we shared our hearts and story, we felt the impact in the room. People were moved. We gave all praise to our Heavenly Father and shared examples of His love that have encouraged our efforts and given us strength to move forward since Ben's suicide. The Holy Spirit within us guided our words to ensure what needed to be said was said, and before we knew it, we were giving thanks to God in our closing.

We promised that faith brings about the transformation they seek. We thanked them for their time with us and ended the presentation with, "God bless." As we did, we heard applause. Terry and I were busy acknowledging each other for a job well done. Imagine our delight and surprise when we looked into the auditorium and noticed our first-ever standing ovation. WOW! We were overwhelmed but reminded of God's promise that we would find goodness in our tragedy. We were witnessing this right before our very own eyes again! Thank you, Jesus! Our God is so good!

7/28/2017

BIG NEWS! Carrie and Matt are engaged! Saturday morning following her engagement, Carrie texted, and we agreed to come and meet up with her for lunch. First, she and Matt are going to the family farm to share the good news with his folks. Getting giddy to think about an upcoming wedding. We had an impromptu engagement party for them with Mandy and Brian at Blackhawk Campground! So fun! Decorated and celebrated! We are so grateful and excited for the blessing of their wedding and Matt becoming our son-in-law. We are also reminded that Benjamin, who would have been so happy for Carrie and Matt, is not here to share in this engagement celebration nor will he be here to celebrate their special wedding day. I appreciate all the well-wishes from people who love and support Carrie and Matt and are excited about their upcoming nuptials! I also find myself wondering if others realize or appreciate the void that can accompany these circumstances. Just a thought.

10/6 & 10/7/2017

Terry and I were invited to a healing grief conference and asked if we'd conduct a workshop for those living in the aftermath of suicide. We agreed. One of the roundtables we attended was facilitated by a woman *from Compassionate Friends, a group for those who've lost children. Participants lost children from ages three to forty from cancer, an accident, or otherwise. As I listened to their stories, I was reminded that many others are going forth on a difficult journey. They wished it had a different outcome. We did, too. But we understand this and know it is possible to march forth and offer the love and faith of Jesus to others who lack hope.*

But they who wait for the Lord shall renew their strength;
they shall mount up with wings like eagles; they shall run and
not be weary; they shall walk and not faint.
Isaiah 40:31 (ESV)

May the God of hope fill you with all joy and peace in believing,
so that by the power of the Holy Spirit you may abound in hope.
Romans 15:13 (ESV)

CHAPTER 8

THE TRAGEDY OF LOSS— THE STRENGTH OF SURVIVAL

*Let us not become weary in doing good, for at the proper time
we will reap a harvest if we do not give up.*
Galatians 6:9 (NIV)

A major part of how my identity as a mother, woman, and human being has changed involves my continuous journey dealing with what I call ***The Tragedy of Loss—The Strength of Survival***. After losing Ben, I contemplated my survival. My path going forward requires perseverance for the obstacles and difficulty ahead. It's a marathon I never trained for from a loss I never anticipated. I'm constantly praying for strength, clinging to hope, practicing gratitude, and seeking God in order to survive.

*Not only so, but we also glory in our sufferings, because we know that
suffering produces perseverance; perseverance, character;
and character, hope. And hope does not put us to shame,
because God's love has been poured out into our hearts
through the Holy Spirit, who has been given to us.*
Romans 5:3-5 (NIV)

As Ben's mom, I wondered if I could go on, if I wanted to, or if it was even possible following his suicide. God was reassuring of His mission for us: bringing light to those in darkness and offering hope in our struggling world. Terry and I agreed to fulfill this mission, one we don't recall signing up for but truly believe God chose us for.

But you are a chosen people, a royal priesthood, a holy nation, God's special possession, that you may declare the praises of Him who called you out of darkness into His wonderful light.
1 Peter 2:9 (NIV)

As the hours, days, months, and years pass, it is becoming more and more apparent that in addition to surviving the tragedy of our loss, it is also crucial to find the strength to move onward without our loved one here. Some days I fail miserably, but I am still standing, still breathing, and still able to move my body and mind in a forward direction. While moving ahead, struggles linger because the thrust to go backward remains in great existence every single day. As Pastor Rick Warren has shared, "If you want to be happy, choose to look at every situation from God's viewpoint." And as stated in Psalm 34:1 (TLB), *"I will praise the Lord no matter what happens."* Being happy is possible, and it's my decision to make each and every day.

If you have children, you can understand the daily rundown of your kids: contemplating what they're up to, what they should be doing—or hoping they're not doing what they shouldn't—their upcoming events, what current challenges they're facing, and when you'll see or hear from them next. As the mom of a deceased child, I can reassure you that I still do this rundown of my kids daily as well. The difference is every time I do, it's a reminder Ben is dead: an agonizing realization. There are still rare instances when something comes up and I think, *Oh, I need to let Ben know about this.* I miss Benjamin each and every day of my life and would give up BENS Hope in an instant to have him back again. But that isn't an option, and because of this realization, I move forward with what is—the BENS Hope ministry that God put on our hearts.

Words cannot express the immense, unconditional love we have for Ben, Mandy, and Carrie. They mean everything to us, as I imagine your kids do as well. I would like to take this opportunity to share something you may or may not be aware of. Having other children does not minimize a loss or, in our case, the pain of losing Ben. We've heard, as other parents have, this specific comment: "Well, you/they have other children." My sister Pam's response to this comment is, "Let me ask, which one of your children could you live without?" Pastor Rick Warren shared a comment his wife Kay made following the death of their son Matthew, who died by suicide in 2013. She asked people to remove the words—AT LEAST during conversations with those who've endured a loss. I concur with Kay.

Another comment expressed to the surviving siblings is, "Be sure to take care of your parents." Please consider what you're saying and asking. I've witnessed how much work Mandy and Carrie have put in for the survival of their own grief and healing journeys let alone being expected to take care of us. I feel these are both examples of knowing what we know based on our circumstances.

Diversions can help keep our reality at bay, and while we welcome life moving forward with BENS Hope and celebrations, events, and travels with the girls that offer normalcy, the reality of Ben's absence remains in my heart. And now back to my journal entries:

10/20/2017

Carrie picked me up for our first excursion to shop for her wedding dress! Needless to say, we were all over the moon with excitement. Mandy met us at a bridal shop for Carrie's first selection. We spent the next two hours taking in rows and rows of dresses and watching Carrie try on dresses. It was awesome! We figured this was probably for the better since the dress options were unlimited and Carrie looked good in every dress: mermaid, trumpet, ballroom, sleek, sexy, and modest styles.

It was also fun seeing Mandy and Brian's furnished apartment—our first visit since we helped them move a couple months ago. After visiting a while, we exchanged goodnights and hugs so Terry and I could get some rest before our early-morning flight to Baltimore for the next nine days of work and pleasure.

10/30/2017

Got home in time to get laundry done and to prepare for another workday. Back to reality tomorrow!

Woke up at 2 a.m. Tried to get back to sleep without success, so I took a quarter tablet of Lorazepam to aid in sleep efforts. Another sleepless hour passed, so I took another quarter tablet, still praying for sleep. Lesson learned today: I will no longer take early-morning appointments. I'm certain my lack of sleep contributed to my morning being filled with tears.

I realized at the Baltimore conference that I'd lost my zest for audits and that God has other plans for me. I'm still waiting to see how this will all play out. For now, my job at the bank is what pays the bills and offers an amazing source of support from some really close friends. That said, being back to work and watching others go on with normal lives while ours is far from normal also brings challenges.

In addition to work doldrums, the third anniversary of Ben's death is around the corner. Regardless of whether one intentionally thinks about that or not, it seems the subconscious is there to remind us of those occurrences.

As I showered and attempted to get dressed for my day, the tears came, as did the uncontrollable sobbing that comes from within the soul. I prayed and prayed for God to help me conquer this sadness and allow me to function today. But that was not meant to be.

I hoped my appointment with Candy would offer some tranquility. At first, it did, but I ended up going through a box of tissues in my puddle of tears. I did learn that I cannot expect support from Terry, Mandy, and Carrie when they are giving what they can but are also in need of support. The people I normally turn to are feeling the same need for solace.

February 2018

A lot of our time and energy has been put toward developing our BENS Hope organization. Our eighty-plus-year-old friend, Mary from Muscoda, introduced us to a man who worked for a coalition from area counties that had funding. He listened to our ideas and what we were proposing to do. We quickly learned that if we wanted to spread the word on suicide prevention, the funding to do this would not come from him but from ourselves.

4/8/2018

Life has been a journey of ups and downs and all-arounds. The good news is we believe in God and are trusting in His plans for us, and we are moving forward since Ben's suicide. We are growing individually, in our marriage, in our family, and most importantly, in our faith.

6/16/2018

We decided to celebrate the girls' birthdays today since both are busy on their actual birthdays. Started the day with a family breakfast at a local favorite, The Owl Cafe: home-cooked goodness! Then Terry headed to pick up two separate birthday cakes, one for each of them! Gram Weigel joined us girls at the local A & M Bridal Boutique where Carrie tried on her chosen wedding dress for the first time! IT LOOKS BEAUTIFUL ON HER, OF COURSE! SO exciting! After some shopping, the girls joined Terry and me at home to discuss BENS Hope. The girls decided to be part of these efforts! Thank you, God! This is a blessing beyond words. We talked about the fourth annual event and graphic design of the poster. Thank you, thank you, thank you, God!

6/22/2018

The girls found a graphic designer. A few emails later and our posters were finally ready to go!

8/3/2018

We delivered the posters around town today, which is also Terry's birthday.

9/1/2018

Vacation time for our thirty-fifth wedding anniversary—Terry and I left for a trip to Chetek. The song "Come as You Are" came on the radio, bringing us both to tears. Ben's song comes our way so often, and it always seems like a sign from him.

As mentioned before, life is hard and not always fair. Even when your intentions are meant to do good, life can throw a wrench into your plans. We're not immune to challenges. Here are some examples leading up to our fourth annual BENS Hope Run/Walk event where our faith was tested:

During our vacation in Chetek, the tooth pain I'd been experiencing these past few months became more intense. The essential oils that were helping the pain subsided and were no longer working. The pain worsened, so I called Platteville Dental and made an appointment. On Monday, I went to the dentist at 10:20 a.m. in Platteville and was transferred to Dubuque for a follow-up at 12:30 p.m. Ended up with a ROOT CANAL on the spot!

On Wednesday, Carrie asked me to go with her to Erschen's Florists and Dubuque to pick up plates and silverware for the wedding, so of course I did. When I came back to town, I ended up back at work, staying late to upload items for the quarterly audit meeting.

Terry was missing Ben; he'd had a bad day and asked to have a glass of wine. My sister, Pam, had also been calling to meet up about the BENS Hope event. I called back, and we talked about that and then some wedding details. Pam ended up coming over around 9 p.m. She was upset and had come from a massage appointment. Apparently, the floodgates of emotions opened from her massage. Later, she started feeling ill and passed out in a lawn chair as we were talking. I couldn't get a pulse, so I called an ambulance. Pam and Bruce were at the hospital until 2:30 a.m. She had suffered from dehydration, exhaustion, and low potassium.

The following week, Terry learned he had shingles. My mom learned she had a torn retina and needed emergency surgery. Seriously?! Talk about Satan meddling in our plans!

Put on the whole armor of God, that you may be able
to stand against the schemes of the devil.
Ephesians 6:11 (ESV)

9/22/2018

Today was the BENS Hope's 4th annual event. As always, Terry, the girls, and I were ready and so appreciative for everyone's work to get us to this day, especially with all the recent challenges ahead of this event. We are always so grateful for our family members who offer their time and energy to make this annual event happen. We could not imagine doing this without them, their love, and support. It means so much. Thank you, God, for blessing us with such a wonderful family.

Following the BENS Hope 5K/2M event, a participant walked over to me and handed me a dollar bill. I looked at them and asked what the dollar was for. He in turn shared that as they walked during the 2M, a man inquired what was going on. The participant shared that they were partaking in a 5K/2M suicide awareness and prevention event. The man said, "It's my last one, but will you give this to the family hosting this event?" He then handed the participant his last dollar bill. WOW!

I remembered a classmate of Carrie's who lost her boyfriend to suicide near the end of their high school years or shortly after graduation. Not sure if or how she dealt with it. Imagine our surprise when this gal showed up at the BENS Hope event this year. How beautiful it is that people are finding the courage to find a safe place to begin dealing with what happened.

It is incredible to see how God is working and touching people through all of this. How blessed are we to be part of it!

October 2018

The weeks leading up to Carrie and Matt's wedding were accompanied by so many highs and lows, it was unbelievable. But it was as God planned, and I kept the faith through all of it!

I'd intended to take off Wednesday through Friday. But as Monday approached, I realized there was much to do. I needed to prepare the house for guests and our hearts and minds for the event. So I took the week off to reintroduce myself to my home and perform the deep cleaning that I'd been accustomed to doing prior to Ben's suicide but not so much since.

As I spent two hours in Ben's bathroom, I realized that I'd gone back in time. I was thinking about the number of times I'd prepared for our kids coming home and spending time with us and the excitement that accompanied that anticipation. As my excitement grew thinking about Carrie and Matt's special occasion, a voice inside reminded me that Ben would not be coming home to share the wedding day with us. The next thing I knew, I was weeping uncontrollably. The depth of pain that I thought had healed once again reared its head in full force. This is now my life?!

After collecting my thoughts and coming back into the reality of this special day, I calmed down with the help of God, of course. God is the constant in my life and puts things into perspective when I cannot. I said a prayer of thanks and continued cleaning. As I made my way throughout the house, I found pictures on a mirror in Mandy's bedroom. There were two each of Ben, Mandy, and Carrie. I decided I should put these in a frame versus having them tucked in the mirror. Shortly after, I found a frame I'd apparently bought at some point. It read, "Moments in time are how memories are made." I marveled at the relevant and impeccable timing of when I located this frame! The frame had openings for three photos; I had two, so I needed one more.

I made my way to the desk where other pictures were gathered, and I picked up the first pile I touched. Of course, they were photos from Ben's funeral. As I looked through the pictures, I saw the beautiful faces of my children as they grew from babies into adults over the years. It seemed like yesterday, and yet, it seemed like forever ago. I was overwhelmed once again that our baby boy, Benjamin, who we once cuddled in our arms as we kissed his precious cheeks and forehead ... our boy who would grow up with so many successes and had so much life ahead, decided to end his life. How could this happen to him? To our family? It's all such deep pain that never ends, and questions always remain. As much as my heart felt sorrowful, this was a week of celebration. And if anyone needed and deserved my full attention, it was Carrie. She was about to be a bride and marry the love of her life, Matt Withrow.

9/21/2019

This is my brother Greg's birthday, and it's also the fifth annual BENS Hope event. Five years! I can hardly believe it. Greg would have turned fifty-two today. Greg was the baby of our family.

Through Ben's death, I found that I was finally allowed to fully grieve the loss of Greg. I wanted to make certain I acknowledged Greg at the BENS Hope fifth annual event and mark the significance of this day. As always, I prayed for another successful BENS Hope 5K/2M event. And it was. Thank you, Jesus! We are blessed by the support and love from friends, family, and our community.

There was a break after the BENS Hope event to gear up for presentations we agreed to do in six new schools: Muscoda, Boscobel, Highland, Dodgeville, Hazel Green, and Shullsburg. We were thankful that our dear friend Mary Grimm of Riverway Communities of Hope sponsored us, and these schools graciously hosted us to aid in suicide awareness/prevention efforts with the encouragement and outreach of Mary.

We feel blessed that God has entrusted us with such an undertaking. We know this is what we were called to do. Our mission of BENS Hope is to reduce the stigma of suicide, aid in suicide awareness/prevention, and offer support and hope to others. Our presentation to students was divinely received. It includes the chicken dance, discussions, and activities addressing kindness, forgiveness, bullying, and social media. It's powerful, and our story of Ben's suicide is shared with vulnerability and honesty. We do this because we want kids to understand that suicide is not the answer. **Suicide is a permanent solution to a temporary situation.**

We can talk with every kid in every class in Platteville, the whole southwestern Wisconsin area, or, for that matter, the world, but nothing will bring Benjamin back. This is a dominant theme in our presentations. There's no second chance. Once you're dead, you're dead. And this is the reality we live with day in and day out and will live with every day for the rest of our lives. We do this because God told us that His Son died to save others and that by us sharing Ben's story, it will save the lives of others.

We hold on to this message and realize that we ourselves cannot save others. But, as God said, our story can. And if our story can be helpful, then that's our ministry, and we'll do what we can to fulfill it. We made presentations almost daily for two weeks, typically two to four a day. It was exhausting and exhilarating. We prayed before, sometimes during, and always after, thanking God for giving us the strength to fulfill His purpose for us. The reactions from the students and faculty are powerful. One of the counselors texted us before we had returned home from a presentation. She said that kids were already coming into her office to talk. One principal told us that teachers and staff at their school witnessed students offering kindness to each other after our visit.

*A school counselor told us that students we'd spoken to went home and shared our visit with their families. They said our visit had truly made an impact on their community. Upon hearing this, I shared it with two friends at work. As the words exited my mouth, I recalled the words God had spoken to me the night of Ben's suicide: **you will find goodness in this**. This is the goodness He had promised more than five years ago. I ended up sobbing from my inner soul, and my friends knelt on either side and held me. I love you, Barb and Sarah.*

11/5/2019: Ben's Angelversary week brought Godwink signs that caught our attention. Terry and I had presentations in Mount Horeb that afternoon. As we pulled into the school parking lot, we noticed that the car next to us was a Honda Civic and the exact same color as Ben's. Of course, we texted a picture to our girls. Carrie's response was, "STOPPP!" Like I always tell others, YOU CAN'T MAKE THIS STUFF UP!

11/21/2019

This morning while walking on the treadmill and praying, I started to see visions on the ceiling. I saw the faces of Jesus, Mary, my dad, my brother Greg, and then Ben's face when he was younger with his big glasses. Then I saw our nephew Tom's face. I gave thanks for our angels among us, the communication of saints Sister Marie told us about, and how God was blessing me in this way.

I felt love and comfort from God. I started singing a song God placed on my heart: "Be not afraid, I go before you always. Come follow me, and I will give you rest." What a beautiful way to start the day. I felt the presence of God and could hear Him speaking to me, offering me comfort and strength.

Terry and I met with Bev, our lawyer friend, who agreed to assist us in establishing BENS Hope Inc. so we can do more to aid suicide awareness/ prevention efforts. We need to select board members. We're praying that our girls will be part of this, but we're not pushing them. My mom agreed to do anything she can to help our efforts. I am also thankful for meeting Teri, a new friend who also lost her son, Jacob, to suicide in 2012. She established Jacob's SWAG Foundation Inc. Teri has given insight to assist our efforts establishing BENS Hope. We're truly blessed by the people the Lord has put on our path as well as His plans for us.

Commit your work to the Lord, and your plans will be established.
Proverbs 16:3 (ESV)

CHAPTER 9

BENS HOPE

In the same way, let your light shine before others, that they may
see your good deeds and glorify your Father in heaven.
Matthew 5:16 (NIV)

BENS Hope's Mission Statement: The BENS Hope Foundation Inc. was created with the intent to offer hope, reduce the stigma of suicide, and aid in suicide awareness and prevention. Our mission is to share Ben's story with people of all ages in communities, schools, and elsewhere. We discuss the sensitive topic of suicide, address bullying, and validate self-worth within each of us. BENS Hope has evolved as a ministry to encourage kindness, forgiveness, healing and provide resources and tools. BENS Hope represents love, care, support, and hope. Because Everyone Needs Some Hope.

You may be asking, how did BENS Hope materialize? I can promise you, this was not on our own accord. We weren't certain we could survive the loss of Benjamin, let alone serve in the capacity we have since his suicide. And it's only by the grace of God we have been able to. I have clung to the words spoken the night of Ben's suicide when I proclaimed, "We will find goodness in this." Those were not my words but words I am certain came from God. We have been obedient, trusting God and His plans for us. BENS Hope transpired from losing Ben and emerged from listening to God, having faith, hope, and patience in Him, and walking with the people He placed on our path.

> For by grace you have been saved through faith. And this is not your own doing; it is the gift of God, not a result of works, so that no one may boast. For we are His workmanship, created in Christ Jesus for good works, which God prepared beforehand, that we should walk in them.
> Ephesians 2:8-10 (ESV)

There's deep meaning and purpose to our BENS Hope organization that Terry came up with, and he says it best: "The story of how I came up with the name for our organization is not a long one, but I believe it is significant. I feel Ben helped me think of the name. We were putting together a walk in Ben's honor, and I also knew we were going to make a website. Ben was always our computer guy, so I know he would have wanted a hand in it. When we were trying to come up with a name for Ben's organization, I thought of what we were trying to do for other people—give hope. The acronym of Ben's name came to me <u>B</u>ecause <u>E</u>veryone <u>N</u>eeds <u>S</u>ome Hope, not only for our family, but for *everyone*." And I couldn't agree more!

We sought support after Ben's death from others who understood and related to losing a loved one to suicide. On the American Foundation for Suicide Prevention (AFSP) website, we located a support group at Journey Mental Health Center in Madison, Wisconsin. Being surrounded by people who experienced a loss to suicide was the best support we could ask for. It took everything in us to walk through those doors when we attended our first meeting. Because of that, we commend everyone who has joined us at a BENS Hope SOS meeting because we know the courage it takes for you to show up, and we applaud you for finding the strength to do so.

We learned the protocol at Journey as the first SOS meeting started. Each attendee introduced themselves, sharing their name, the name and relationship of their deceased loved one, when their loved one died, and how they took their life. I recall a couple of things that came to mind. First, one of the attendees mentioned their loss happening thirteen years ago. My immediate thought was, *God, please let me be healed before thirteen years pass.* What I realize now is that these survivors may not just be there for their own purpose, but to benefit us as new attendees. And this reassurance is needed! Because for anyone who has experienced a loss, their new reality can seem impossible. What I do know is while I moved forward from other losses, the loss of my child completely transformed me and changed who I was, and I'll never be the person that I was before he died. It's just not possible.

I also questioned the need for sharing *how* Ben took his life. My actual thought was, *It's none of their damn business.* But as I sat and listened to other attendees recite how their loved one died by suicide, I realized we weren't the only ones in these shoes. There were others impacted by the tragedy of losing their loved one to suicide as well. It was a blessing to realize that others cared and understood. We didn't have to carry our burden alone.

Carry each other's burdens, and in this way
you will fulfill the law of Christ.
Galatians 6:2 (NIV)

What I want to share with any other survivor is that as painful and difficult as it was to find the courage and capacity to spill my heart and tears out with strangers, it was truly my saving grace. It may be for you too. I found comfort in the company of others who understood the depths of this tragedy. Suicide is a unique beast and was unlike any other loss I had previously experienced. The members of the support group listened without judgment and communicated with love and compassion through their words and through their eyes. It was a safe place for all of us to share feelings that surfaced. While the tears came endlessly at times, so did the unconditional love of the participants. It was and still is an incredible experience to know this support is available.

As Terry and I experienced the benefits of these support meetings, we pondered the idea of starting a group. Our prayers validated this need to offer support locally. We revisited the AFSP website and purchased the materials to become peer facilitators of an SOS group to be offered in southwest Wisconsin. A facilitator at Journey Mental Health expressed her concerns for us facilitating a peer SOS group. She suggested we wait for time to pass, saying there were more books to be read. We appreciated and listened to her concerns, which were valid. However, we ultimately followed what God had brought before us, doing what He guided us to do. In March 2015, four months following Ben's suicide, we hosted our first SOS with twenty-five people in attendance. We are honored to offer this support and feel it's a reminder that with God all things are possible.

☼

Jesus looked at them and said, "With man this is impossible,
but with God all things are possible."
Matthew 19:26 (NIV)

Please know that you are not alone! BENS Hope support is available in southwest Wisconsin the second Tuesday of each month. Check out afsp.org to find a suicide-bereavement support group near you.

It was shortly after Ben's suicide when Jenny introduced us to Meghan, her church friend. Meghan had placed a devotion in the prayer basket at church explaining her desire to help others struggling or impacted by suicide, due to her own related struggles. When Jenny shared this, my initial thought was, *Are you serious*?! But that's our amazing God! As He brought Meghan into our lives, there came more introductions, interactions, and opportunities. One of the individuals Meghan introduced to us was another amazing lady, Barb. She is an incredible lady who founded and is the executive director of the Center for Suicide Awareness in Kaukauna, Wisconsin. Little did we know how our lives would intertwine and how instrumental Barb would become in our efforts creating BENS Hope.

Initially, BENS Hope had no funding. Everything we hosted, whether speaking engagements, meetings for SOS on campus at UW-Platteville, or our community SOS group, we offered out of the goodness of our hearts. Our mission was purely to share our story in the hopes of reducing the stigma of suicide and aid in suicide awareness and prevention. We took every opportunity to present to local clubs, groups, and organizations that were interested in hearing us share Ben's story, and this outreach remains a priority.

In September 2015, ten months following Benjamin's suicide, we hosted the first BENS Hope 5K/2M Suicide Awareness and Prevention event with our faith, help from Meghan and Barb, and the tremendous support of our family members on hand. We were astonished that this came to fruition in this short of a time period. It was a huge success! A minimal fee was charged and included a meal and T-shirt. I guess this was actually our first official BENS Hope fundraiser. We continue to host this event each September.

Outside of the annual 5K/2M event, there are no other current BENS Hope fundraisers. I guess between our three kids, I've had my share of fundraising over the years. However, as the years have gone by and requests have increased for school presentations and additional speaking engagements, we now charge a fee to compensate our efforts and offset expenses.

We are blessed and thankful for the donations we receive. I've shared with Terry that this money is not ours: it's just money we will recycle and bless others with. God continues to put ideas in our minds and on our hearts with ways we can help others. In addition to the annual BENS Hope 5K/2M event and monthly SOS meetings, we host a BENS Hope Helping Hands event. God put this event on Terry's heart five years after Ben's suicide. It was the middle of the night when he awoke and received specific instructions on it. Terry agreed it was a great idea but didn't take time to write anything down even after God told him to do so. Terry reassured God he wouldn't forget, but God was persistent, and Terry was obedient and got out of bed to write these details on paper. Of course, our family was amazed by this idea when Terry shared it with us the following morning! It entails accepting nominations during the month of February on our Facebook page and on bens-hope.org. Individuals can nominate someone they feel has blessed others with their kindness, someone who is down on their luck, or a student furthering their education in a mental-health-related field. From these nominations, three are chosen, and each is blessed with a monetary donation. The selected nominees are announced March 5, which is Ben's birthday. Such a wonderful way to remember Ben and support our community that continues to bless us. This event is well received and appreciated!

I also host BENS Hope Healing Hearts retreats for moms who have lost a child by suicide or otherwise. Interested participants provide a deposit to reserve their spot. This deposit also holds them accountable for showing up. The first year, Matt Melby and Justin Erickson, two funeral directors, co-sponsored this event while Mandy and Carrie co-hosted it with me. Even with just three other moms at the first retreat, the experience was so powerful! I recall those moms bravely showing up, sharing how they had contemplated not coming but were so grateful they did! At the second retreat I hosted in the fall of 2022, Sister Kay and Sister Marie kindly welcomed the guests, showing the moms to their respective rooms at Sisters of the Presentation before everyone gathered in the dining room for a lovely meal. A tour of the venue followed before we met up in our conference room for the opening ceremony, a heartfelt experience to participate in and witness. Our time together included sharing our hearts, tears, laughter, and self-reflection, along with taking advantage of journaling opportunities. Sessions to date have included meditations, massages, breathing exercises, art therapy, reflexology, and plate smashing, which is quite therapeutic! Let me just say, you'll want to stand back when you give these mommas a hammer.

But in all seriousness, I am humbled and honored to lead these grief retreats. It is beautiful to witness honest conversations, vulnerability, and breakthroughs, as well as become acquainted with these warrior moms as they share memories of their deceased child/children. Whether their losses were months or decades ago, these moms offer understanding and empathy to each other. It is heart filling. From my personal loss, I will share that while my pain has softened over time, my *yearning* for Ben remains. The desire for his presence, his kindness, his support, and the reflection on what could have been still lingers. These retreats run Friday night through noon on Sunday. Following the closing ceremony on Sunday, the attendees' deposits are returned ahead of their leaving. It's incredible to learn of their hesitation to attend and amazing to witness their desire to stay as the retreat comes to a close. It is truly a tremendous experience and a privilege to offer these retreats free to moms, due to the blessing of donations received through BENS Hope. I look forward to hosting additional retreats in the future.

Additionally, donations received through BENS Hope are dispersed for insurance costs, materials for events we host or attend, and resource materials used for our school presentations, including silicone bracelets, pens, and safety crisis plan cards, all inscribed with crisis numbers. We also donated 600 bracelets to a family who was in a local parade. They had lost their child to suicide and wanted to promote suicide awareness at the parade. Other expenses covered include community and campus SOS meetings, counseling costs for survivors, provided clothing or food, and materials offered to aid in postvention efforts. We also started offering scholarships to students furthering their education in a mental-health-related field.

BENS Hope functions as an extension of our family. Currently, our board members consist of our immediate family and our friend and lawyer, Bev, who assisted us in setting up our nonprofit. In establishing BENS Hope, we became independent from the Center for Suicide Awareness (CSA). We greatly appreciate all the assistance and support we've received and extend our sincerest gratitude to Barb and the CSA for their contributions in our development of BENS Hope Inc.

When we launched BENS Hope, we came together as a family to determine what was needed to put our message and mission out into the world. When it came to creating our social media presence, I thought, *Hmmm...Ben was our tech guy, so how are we going to make this happen?* As God would have it, Ben's friend, Mike, assisted us by creating a website, which we greatly appreciated! After Mike moved to another state, we were blessed through Barb and met Justin Jahns of JahnsTek, who revamped our website: www.bens-hope.org. Words cannot express our gratitude for Justin, whose kindness mirrors Benjamin's. He's always available to answer questions, help with requests, and offer guidance. Justin is truly a godsend! I encourage you to check out JahnsTek if you need assistance with IT. Mandy and Carrie assisted in revamping our BENS Hope brochures and our BENS Hope branding. We came up with the slogan: *Connect, Support, Grieve, Heal—You Are Not Alone.* This is more than just a slogan for BENS Hope; these four words and the mantra of "You are not alone" are words we live by each and every day.

Looking back, two occasions come to mind that seemed to initiate our speaking engagements and outreach efforts through BENS Hope. We never know how one opportunity will ignite others! The first involved Meghan, or her absence in this case. Meghan had invited us to attend a meeting with her in Darlington for the Children's Health Alliance committee. This group noticed suicide creeping into their numbers, and they were interested in hearing our story. Unfortunately, Meghan, a new mommy, had to cancel at the last minute, so we were on our own. Terry and I were nervous attending without Meghan. She had been our crutch, and up to this point, typically spoke on our behalf at meetings or events because we didn't have the capacity to at that time. Terry and I attended the meeting as planned, which went extremely well. As we told our story, there was not a dry eye in the room. We shared how we were blindsided by Ben's decision to take his life and how life as we knew it changed in an instant! What came next shocked us. Members of the committee asked, "What are you doing to aid in suicide prevention?" *WHAT?! Were they serious?!* Didn't they know that it took everything—body, mind, and soul—for us to be in that room? Couldn't they see our wounded hearts after just listening to our story, still so fresh from Ben's suicide?! Now they felt compelled to ask what we were doing to prevent it? We were baffled and in total disbelief. This ask had not crossed our minds, but my belief is that there is a reason for everything. God had planted the seed because He knew He had much more in store for us.

The second instance occurred November 8, 2016, at our monthly SOS meeting. As referenced in my journal entries in Chapter 6, two sixth-grade students in junior high, Cooper and Bristol, joined us along with Bristol's mom. The students had experienced losses of loved ones to suicide, but their attendance came with more intentions than we initially realized. They shared with the group that they had hosted a haunted house at one of their family's farms over Halloween and wanted to donate the money they raised to BENS Hope and asked if we could help them. Inquisitive, we wondered how. Their response was startling. They said that they had friends who thought suicide was the answer to their problems. We were mortified! *Suicide is the answer? Why would they think this?* Because we only know what we know.

We reassured them that *suicide is not the answer* and that there is help for those struggling. We asked the students to talk with the administrators at their school to see if we could visit and speak with their friends. Thank you, God, and bless the Platteville Middle School and especially Vicki Feldman for listening to the concerns of these students and inviting us in to speak on the topic of suicide. It is our mission to ensure students understand that suicide is not the answer but that *suicide is a permanent solution to a temporary situation.* And we want to ensure everyone reading this book understands too! There are no do-overs or second chances when this decision is made. Once you're dead, you're dead. Our intent is not to glorify suicide but to focus on what the reality of being a survivor looks and feels like firsthand.

You have to admire these courageous sixth graders who spoke up about concerns for their friends and how their efforts may have contributed to saving the lives of others. Because of their concerns and actions, they became the gateway for BENS Hope visiting schools. And because of their initial outreach, we have made countless presentations reaching thousands of students. To honor these two, during the eighth annual BENS Hope 5K/2M event in 2022, we recognized Cooper and Bristol—now freshmen at UW-Platteville. Each received a scholarship from BENS Hope toward their education. Bristol plans to major in business and Cooper in psychology. We extend a sincere thank you for the difference they have already made in this world and wish them all the best in their future endeavors.

BENS Hope would not be the organization it is today if we didn't have the love and support of our family and friends. We are indebted to their length of participation, their contributions, support, insight, direction, guidance, and the list goes on and on. Our family is so gracious, and not only do they participate annually in the BENS Hope 5K/2M events, but they selflessly volunteer their time overseeing areas that are key to the success of this event. This ranges from helping with traffic control, managing the food line, making pickups and deliveries, filling and distributing balloons, putting up and taking down tents, helping other volunteers get to their designated areas, and the list goes on. We simply cannot thank them enough. Family, we love you!

Another amazing volunteer who has been a constant and always supportive of us and our family is my mom, Ann. She graciously donates her time, energy, and more. She attends SOS meetings to support us and attends events in our absence to represent BENS Hope. Outside of our social media efforts, she elects to deliver posters around southwest Wisconsin for the annual BENS Hope event. She's our loyal spokesperson promoting BENS Hope, supporting us, and remembering her grandson, Ben. She's always there to lend a helping hand, offer a shoulder to cry on, or put forth a listening ear or a warm embrace to us, other attendees, or strangers she meets. She's blessed numbers of people who have shared their stories on how suicide has impacted their lives. She's a tremendous support to many!

In addition to Mom's tremendous kindness and generosity, and, as referenced to earlier, we were blessed with another extraordinary senior, Mary Grimm. We met our dear friend Mary in 2018 while attending a health coalition meeting with five counties represented.

Mary had it in her heart, as did we, to help others struggling and in need of support and hope. We had both attended this meeting with the anticipation that we may be considered for funding to aid in our respective outreach efforts. Sadly, we were not considered for funding, which was so unfortunate when it was on our hearts to help.

However, a few weeks later, Terry and I received an invite from Mary. We made the drive to her country home, which seemed to be out in the middle of nowhere. Upon our arrival, we were welcomed by Mary and her daughter, Marge, with open arms. After an enjoyable lunch, Mary reached behind her, locating a paper she in turn handed to me. As I glanced at the first few words, my eyes filled with tears. Mary was sharing the same poem I read regularly at that time. It's "The Tapestry Poem" by Corrie ten Boom, too beautiful not to share with you now.

The Tapestry Poem

My life is but a weaving
Between my God and me.
I cannot choose the colors
He weaveth steadily.

Oft' times He weaveth sorrow;
And I in foolish pride
Forget He sees the upper
And I the underside.

Not 'til the loom is silent
And the shuttles cease to fly
Will God unroll the canvas
And reveal the reason why.

The dark threads are as needful
In the weaver's skillful hand
As the threads of gold and silver

In the pattern He has planned

He knows, He loves, He cares;
Nothing this truth can dim.
He gives the very best to those
Who leaves the choice to Him.

It has been some time since I have read this poem. But reading it again as I'm writing this book, I recall clinging to this poem with such hope and trust in God's plans. This poem meant so much then and still resonates now. The power of these words carried me through some of my darkest days. This poem also offered a flicker of hope that I desperately needed. May it bless you also.

Our friendship with Mary blossomed over the years. She was influential in reaching out to schools in various districts, asking them to consider our BENS Hope message on suicide prevention. While all of our school presentations are special, one from 2018 holds a special memory. It was our visit to Boscobel because Marge, Mary's daughter, brought Mary to see us! They came to witness firsthand the power behind our BENS Hope suicide awareness/prevention presentations. Mary knew our words came from not just talking the talk but walking the walk every day as survivors of suicide. Mary herself was a survivor, so she absolutely understood the magnitude of our efforts. After finishing up our presentation in the school auditorium, we walked over to where Mary was seated. She extended her hands into mine and locked eyes with me as tears welled up in hers. Mary thanked us for being obedient to God's plans and agreeing to proceed with the BENS Hope ministry, educating on suicide prevention and offering hope to those struggling.

Mary was a believer and a prayer warrior. Each phone call we engaged in always ended in prayer. I miss our talks, her laugh, and the opportunity to pray with her. Mary was united with God on October 1, 2021. I think of her often, feel her guidance, and know she's still cheering me on as I take on my new role as a grief, grace, and gratitude specialist in my next chapter of life.

His master replied, 'Well done, good and faithful servant! You have been faithful with a few things; I will put you in charge of many things. Come and share your master's happiness!
Matthew 25:23 (NIV)

CHAPTER 10

BENS HOPE EDUCATION FOR STUDENTS AND ADULTS

You, however, are not in the realm of the flesh but are in the realm of the
Spirit, if indeed the Spirit of God lives in you. And if anyone does
not have the Spirit of Christ, they do not belong to Christ.
Romans 8:9 (NIV)

We wish we were given the topic of unicorns and butterflies, but we got the topic of suicide based on our circumstances. We take suicide seriously and are passionate about talking about it. Why? Because our son died by suicide, and we don't want this to happen to you! We believe God chose us for this ministry. He didn't say we'd like it, and God didn't say it would be easy, but He did promise to walk with us every step of the way, and, of course, He is.

When initially considering the requests for school visits, Terry and I had a lot of anxiety about presenting to students since our previous audience had only been adults. We prayed a lot and talked with God as well. I was feeling frantic, nervous, and overwhelmed. I distinctly recall riding my bike one morning and discussing with God about being scared to address the topic of suicide with these kids. It terrified me to think about what would happen if a student did end up actually killing him/herself?! God made it *instantly* clear that *we* do not have the power to save anyone! That is His doing! Terry's and my responsibility is only to share Ben's story, which God reassured us will save lives.

Our agenda for student presentations was divinely orchestrated and put on our hearts by God. It is relevant to our audience, addresses extremely important topics, offers our personal experience, and delivers a compelling message. While the agenda is the same, each presentation style varies based on our audience and the guidance from the Holy Spirit we receive while we are presenting. As Pastor Rick Warren has shared, "We choose to do the right thing in situations and then trust God's Spirit to give us His power, love, faith, and wisdom to do it. Since God's Spirit lives inside of us, these things are always available for the asking." He offers further confirmation in this scripture: *"For God is working in you, giving you the desire and the power to do what pleases Him."* Philippians 2:13 (NLT, second edition)

Teachers who have witnessed our presentations can validate this as well. I've had teachers tell me that the message we delivered was presented in exactly the manner the classroom of students needed to hear it. Such a powerful testimony of God's power and will. Thy will be done!

Our presentation begins with an icebreaker that allows us to interact with the students and start on a lighter note, followed by the music video for "Why" by Rascal Flatts, which sets the stage for our presentation. The reactions from the students during this video introduction give us a better idea of our classroom audience. Terry stands in the front of the classroom since he presents immediately following the video. I wander to the back of the classroom and get situated. As the video plays, I silently pray for the students, most of whom I've never met, but I know they are someone's child, grandchild, or loved one. I ask God to please anoint our minds and mouths so the message we convey stays with these students. I pray with all my heart their families will never know the pain of losing their child to suicide. As the video wraps up, I return to the front of the classroom, *always* emotional and reminded of what brought us to this moment, *our son Ben's suicide.*

In addition to the video, our presentation includes lessons, activities, and resources. The biggest lesson in sharing Ben's story is the permanence of his suicide and the aftermath on survivors. In addition to suicide, we also address social media and bullying, which wasn't on our radar but was on God's agenda. These topics piggyback into the topics of kindness and forgiveness. Activities include an exercise called "Let It Go." We hand out note cards, asking the students to anonymously write down something that is weighing heavily on their hearts—maybe something that was done to them by someone else or maybe something they've done to another person. As they write on this card, we ask them to reflect, ask for forgiveness or offer forgiveness, and then to release this weight and let it go. We share that the pain they carry will be with them forever unless they can find it in their hearts to offer forgiveness for themself or the other person involved. We know there are root causes of pain for students (and adults), and it is important to deal with them to avoid deeper pain, which can contribute to emotional, mental, or physical pain and even suicidal thoughts. As noted by John Hopkins Medicine:

Whether it's a simple spat with your spouse or long-held resentment toward a family member or friend, unresolved conflict can go deeper than you may realize—it may be affecting your physical health. The good news: studies have found that the act of forgiveness can reap huge rewards for your health, lowering the risk of heart attack, improving cholesterol levels and sleep, and reducing pain, blood pressure, and levels of anxiety, depression, and stress. And research points to an increase in the forgiveness-health connection as you age.

We hope that this "Let It Go" exercise benefits students as they offer this act of forgiveness. If you feel it would be beneficial in your life, we encourage you to utilize it as well.

Terry and I had no idea what might be weighing on the hearts of these students but wanted to share some of the responses we received:

I want the fighting in my family to stop. It hurts every time to hear all the yelling and shouting every night, and I can't do anything about it.

I never bullied someone, but several times in my life I have been told to kill myself because I was too fat or because of my background. This is hard to take in. I get told to kill myself in person and online.

When I was in fourth grade a girl told me to shoot myself in the head at the tetherball spot during recess.

My friends make fun of me and question my sexuality.

My mom doesn't accept me for my sexuality, and my dad tells me it's a mental illness.

I want to forgive myself for all the damage I have done to my skin and for trying to end everything when there is so much more I can do to fix myself and my mental health.

The time I was at work and didn't give the person the right change, I felt really bad.

I told my sibling that I hated them when they were struggling, I didn't think.

Racist comments some people say to me.

Free from anxiety, depression, and guilt and to love myself.

I assumed this person said something nasty about my friend, and I called them a very inappropriate name, and now we haven't spoken in over two years. I regret it so much.

Someone told me no one loves me and if I was gone no one would care.

I let my friend go through her struggles even though she voiced them to me.

Someone told me to go die in a hole. That really hurt me.

Abused me, broke me, hit me, and screamed at me.

My mom puts me down, calls me names, hits me, and gave me away.

I wish I was nicer and didn't make those comments, I'm sorry.

I have taken personal property.

I need to forgive someone for leaving, and I need to let go of words they said to me.

I do things I shouldn't, but I do things to make people laugh.

I was told I was ugly and would never be anything. I was told to disappear.

My dad died, he killed himself.

I know someone killed herself two months ago. I couldn't save her.

My dad tried killing himself when I was in fourth grade, and I've never been the same since. I'm traumatized.

My birth father beat me when I was younger, I'll never forgive him.

My dad makes me hold up our family with his dying heart. I forgive him.

I struggle with the pressures that teachers put on students to get good grades and be good students. Sometimes teachers are the bullies. (Written by a teacher.)

Who would have known eighth graders could be carrying such weight on their shoulders? While it may not come as a surprise to some of you, it was heart-wrenching and definitely eye-opening to us. Raw emotions rose to the surface, not just because of our son's suicide but because of the personal pain those kids had been bottling up within themselves. Do any of these items resonate? Do we send our kids or grandkids out the door each morning and wish them a good day? Do we really know what's on their hearts? Are we asking them or assuming we know? Are we aware of any struggles or pain they're facing? Are they being bullied? Are they the bully? Have we heard that kids who get picked on have been involved in school shootings? Have we heard that kids getting bullied have died by suicide? What are we doing to resolve whatever "it" is, or are we contributing to it? These are just some important thoughts I ask each of us to ponder.

We are thankful for the kids that shared their hearts, and we pray they find forgiveness and hope in their circumstances. We also thank the teachers and counselors who utilized these anonymous responses to benefit their respective classrooms and students, reassuring them that others are dealing with similar challenges and that they are not alone.

Another classroom exercise is preparing a safety and crisis plan. This idea actually came to us from UW-Platteville college students (we offered bimonthly support on campus). Because the majority of students we integrated with dealt with suicidal ideations and had a safety and crisis plan, they encouraged us to prepare plans with the students we visited in schools, so we did just that! During one of our presentations, I was directing the students to write down the names of two contacts they could reach out to, and a student asked, "What if you don't feel you have anyone you can reach out to?" Again, my heart dropped. Since that interaction, I've reassured the students that they can contact me to assist them in finding the help they need, and I have been taken up on my offer. If you question how sincere our intentions are to aid in suicide prevention, hopefully this offers insight and validates that we care about you and your loved ones.

As hard as it is to repeat our story of losing Ben to suicide, we know the power it has and the impact it's making. God put it on our hearts to share Ben's story because He said by doing so, it will save lives. We pray our efforts reduce the stigma of suicide and offer support and hope to others by letting them know they do matter in this world and we care about them. While we are aware of the resistance and hesitation some have about our visits, now is an opportune time to share some of the students' takeaways following our classroom presentations:

I liked how it gave options for getting help and talked about how everyone experiences these types of thoughts once in a while throughout their lifetime. I think that this would be very useful to someone who thought that they were struggling alone.

That suicide is not simply killing yourself. Your life is not wholly your own, it belongs also to the people you love, and when you die, a part of them dies also. I didn't understand that until after the presentation.

That this is a real thing and it really hurts the people you leave behind, so think about who you're going to hurt before you do it.

Suicide is not the answer. There is help, so get it. There are people there to help you. They want to help you.

I thought it was a great presentation for perspective, and it made me think. It was well put together and was a very good experience. I'm thankful they came to talk with us.

That it is OK to not be OK and that if you are struggling you should seek help and not be ashamed of it. Everyone struggles at some point; I didn't always believe that before this presentation.

I thought it was pretty powerful and also very helpful for people who are struggling with mental health issues.

I liked that they were honest, no beating around the bush, no sugar coating. This is their story, and they told it how it is. It was a very powerful presentation, sad, but powerful.

I liked how they were supportive and told us we could talk to them if we had no one.

I liked how influential the presentation was and informational.

Information and ideas. The crisis response cards were an amazing and smart idea.

The Cullens actually know what they are talking about, and you get to see how this changed their lives forever! It reminds you that taking your life doesn't only affect you, it affects everyone that loves and cares about you!

During COVID-19, rather than making onsite school visits, we offered virtual presentations. Mandy and Carrie also joined these classrooms virtually. The students prepared questions for us, which the teacher provided to us ahead of each visit. We were able to offer insight based on our personal experiences and covered topics they requested. Those included mindfulness, self-care, depression, stress, and anxiety. We also discussed their effects on the body and mind. Students inquired on how to best support a family member or friend. We provided resources and techniques we've learned and utilized, especially since Ben's suicide. We understand the impact that COVID-19 had and the struggles that accompanied it. They are real. Your feelings are valid. Please reach out for help and know you're not alone.

For those concerned about our classroom visits, hopefully these testimonies offer insight. Another comment often shared by teachers and SOS attendees is, "I never thought about how suicide would impact my parents, grandparents, siblings, etc." We're confident they will now. I hope and pray that instead of feeling fearful of talking about suicide, you can see the impact of our visits and the benefits of our efforts through BENS Hope.

Below is additional affirmation of our presentation and its lasting impression. This testimony was shared by a middle school teacher:

I would just like to thank you guys again for coming and talking to our students. On Thursday and Friday when I had those classes, I had planned to have a ten-minute discussion on your presentation and get their thoughts and feedback about it. That conversation took our class's entire forty-five minutes in all three classes. They had so many good things to say about it, and they got so much out of it. All of the classes wanted me to thank you guys for coming and for doing this for them and all of the other people that you guys talk to and help each day. So thank you one more time for coming and talking to us about your story and sharing information!

And the superintendent's letter:

Dear Mr. and Mrs. Cullen,

On behalf of the Mount Horeb Area School District, I offer my deepest gratitude for sharing with our faculty and staff your story of profound loss and extraordinary resiliency. You taught us, among other things, the pathway to healing is through channeling our grief in service to others. It is difficult to comprehend the fact that several beautiful children will not be returning to our classrooms this week. As a community, we have been reeling. A malaise has hung over Mount Horeb. It is palpable. That changed when you took the microphone and shared your personal experiences. We needed to heal. We needed to know there is a way forward. No one but you could have provided that sense of hope. As importantly, your insightful presentation has given our staff license to have courageous conversations about suicide. No longer can it be acceptable to simply explain away these deaths as "unexpected." Like your beautiful Ben, each of these souls were contending with deep pain. In many instances, that profound anguish is too often masked for fear of societal stigmas. You reminded us the importance of moving discussions past the façade of a "brave" face to conversations which reflect the multi-layered realities of peoples' lives. Your inspirational back-to-school kickoff message moved our school community from a "post-vention" mindset to prevention. While words cannot possibly begin to express my sincerest condolences for the extensive loss you have endured, your fortitude in sharing your experiences exemplifies the very message you imparted on those assembled: be kind to one another, talk about suicide, and educate to demystify stigmas. The work you put into making us better is not lost on me. Our students, staff, and community will be the benefactors of your exemplary efforts.

With warmest regards,

Dr. Steve Salerno , Superintendent

For more testimonials, please feel free to visit bens-hope.org.

The adults who have witnessed our presentation encourage us to share with every student at every school! But obviously this decision is not ours to make. While we have spoken in large group or assembly settings at UW-Platteville and Southwest Technical College, our visits in junior and senior high schools have been made in individual classrooms. You may ask why, since doing one presentation would take less time than making multiple presentations, right? Well, it's because we don't do these presentations just to say we did. We do these presentations because we truly want to ensure our visits aid in suicide awareness and prevention when we talk with these kids, your loved ones! We want to be close enough to look them in the eye and ensure they understand the sincerity of our visit and witness the brokenness of our hearts since Ben made the decision to take his life. We want them to see what we feel, and we offer the most compelling presentation possible. If we're going to pour our hearts out to make a lasting impact, we want to have their undivided attention.

As much as we appreciate and understand the importance of our visits to classrooms to talk with students, we appreciate talking with faculty and staff. Who better to have the conversation with than those who spend the majority of time with our kids and grandkids, right?

Our desire to speak to such groups, we believe, will aid in suicide awareness and prevention. We know of a teacher who was alarmed after reading a school project one of her students completed. This teacher took action, and their efforts very well may have saved this student's life. In another school-related situation, rather than action being taken, excuses were made, and the incident was swept under the rug. This family was not as fortunate; the student took their life.

We pray if people can learn from our experience, it can save them from going through it. Will you put your concerns for your loved one ahead of your fear and learn from our story? We're here for you! Do we know everything about suicide? Absolutely not. Does anyone? Not that we've met. While we don't have all the answers, we do know more than we did prior to November 11, 2014. I feel the topic of suicide should be a priority. Why? Because it's frustrating when people jump on the bandwagon feeling bad following a suicide loss, and it leaves me wondering what actions were taken to prevent it. Let me give you this to ponder. Would you rather be on the proactive side of suicide or reactive? Think about it, please. Regardless, BENS Hope will be here for you either way.

I recall when I was younger people avoided the topic of cancer, and it was referred to by some as the the "C" word. People avoided it at all costs! Why? Because cancer might involve death. But as years have gone by, cancer has become discussed more openly, and that's a good thing. This is what we want for suicide as well—to talk about it openly and to normalize the conversation so if someone wants to bring up the topic of suicide, they can without feeling alienated or judged.

The stigma surrounding suicide definitely impedes what we're trying to achieve with our message and mission of suicide prevention. Terry and I have no reservations sharing our story. Some people are hesitant in promoting our efforts because they have a false idea that talking about suicide will glorify suicide. It's a fact that talking about suicide provides the opportunity for communication. It can also diminish fears and encourage conversations on feelings. Please note that the act of suicide is not our focus, the pain for us as survivors is.

Interestingly enough, once that initial conversation occurs, the next one becomes easier as walls come down, gradually alleviating any fear to explore this topic. This is exactly what happened when I spoke to a high school principal. He invited us to come talk with his faculty and staff about suicide. He told me that just by engaging in a conversation with us prior to our visit, he found his mind at ease and anxiety reduced. Some more insight for you to ponder.

We want faculty, staff, parents, grandparents, families, and others to know that regardless of whether they as adults want to talk about suicide or not, kids *are* talking about it. We are graciously offering our real-life experience to educate on a topic we never anticipated experiencing but did so anyway. And we can promise that you don't want to live in this nightmare that you cannot wake up from. Talk about suicide. It could be the difference between life and death.

There are obviously a lot of different scenarios about how the outcome of our lives could have played out after losing Ben. The fact that we are still here and want to offer hope to others is validation of God's hand in our journey to fulfill the mission He put upon us. And every time we leave a school, we think, *we know it's only by the grace of God we are serving in this capacity.*

※

But I say to you, love your enemies and
pray for those who persecute you.
Matthew 5:44 (ESV)

※

Therefore encourage one another and build
another up, just as you are doing.
1 Thessalonians 5:11 (ESV)

CHAPTER 11

BENS HOPE—SOS

Blessed be the God and Father of our Lord Jesus Christ, the Father of
mercies and God of all comfort, who comforts us in all our affliction, so
that we may be able to comfort those who are in any affliction, with the
comfort with which we ourselves are comforted by God.
2 Corinthians 1:3-4 (ESV)

Aside from presentations, an equally important part of BENS Hope
is our SOS group meetings, which we are honored to host. We've
learned that once you establish a group where people feel safe and can
speak freely without judgment, there is a mutual trust shared among
survivors. I honestly admire the courageous attendees who show up,
put in the hard work of getting uncomfortable and being vulnerable,
and deal with the pains of their loss. I believe that moving through
these feelings contributes to the healing we are seeking.

Over my years of participating in SOS meetings, I've found myself
reflecting on Ben's suicide and comparing his to other stories that are
shared with us. Listening to the logistics of what some have experienced
in their suicide loss adds to the trauma of an already heart-wrenching
event. These conversations take me back to the graphic stories shared
by survivors in Carla Fine's book: images of people struggling to save
their loved one, witnessing their loved one take their life in their
presence, breaking wrists and ankles trying to save their loved one,
wrestling over a gun, or being the person to come upon their loved one

following the suicide. My heart goes out to each of them. I'm so sorry.

Regardless of what end of the spectrum we're sitting on, whether struggling or a survivor, I believe our conversations at SOS are invaluable and contribute to each other. We talk, we share, we learn, and we care in a way that others cannot comprehend. We put in the work to move forward one day at a time. And it doesn't matter how many times we fall; what matters is that we keep getting up and moving forward knowing that we are not alone and that others care. While we cannot walk your journey for you, we are here to walk it with you.

I understand being inquisitive when we learn of another's suicide. First are the feelings of shock that accompany a loss. Following are the inevitable questions:

Why?

What happened?

How are their loved ones?

Where were their loved ones?

How did they take their life?

What went wrong?

What part did others play in their decision?

As humans, our curiosity drives us to explanations. Whether one is a child or an adult, we seek answers to our questions. In cases such as this, regardless of what questions are answered or not, the outcome remains the same: our loved one is dead, and we're left to deal with this horrific reality, and there is no guidebook to help us navigate through this tragedy. A comment we frequently heard following Ben's suicide was, "I don't know what to say." I just want to take this opportunity to share that we didn't know what to say either. We weren't given a book after Ben's suicide that offered answers to our questions or yours. That's just a thought for you to ponder. What did help me profusely was when people offered a listening ear. It was and still is a wonderful way for you to validate your support without words, without judgement and blame. I also welcomed hugs and now find myself offering hugs to others every opportunity I get. They are powerful! When you give a hug, you receive one in return. It's a double blessing.

Additional insight I wish to share is there is much more to a person than the act of suicide itself. Here are some thoughts to ponder before you mark the identity of survivors or loved ones exclusively to suicide. Please know that Ben did not have our consent for his decision to take his life, and I would imagine most survivors don't. Please understand that while Ben's suicide is the final memory to many, it does not define who Benjamin was as a person nor does it define who we are as a family. Consider, like we do, the fact that Ben was our sweet baby boy who grew up into a wonderful and successful young man. He paid attention to conversations, and his gift giving reflected this. He loved giving! His ideas were some of the best ever! He was thoughtful, kind, and selfless. He gave without ever requesting anything in return. He was loyal to his employers, friends, and family. He loved his family! He loved hanging out with his friends. He enjoyed gaming and excursions with the guys to the cabin. Please know there is *so much more* to our loved ones than suicide. There are all the other events we remember and look back on with fondness. We have memories we will cherish, and we will forever miss our loved ones. Yes, there is much more to our loved ones than the act that ended their lives.

While nothing was off the table for our family conversations, I can honestly say I don't recall any specific discussions on suicide outside of hearing of someone's loss and feeling bad for them. Our conversations still encompassed all topics imaginable. Ask our girls. No topics were off limits. Suicide wasn't one we contemplated, but we didn't think we needed to. Now our wish is that we would have.

For those who think talking about suicide will encourage suicide, that is a myth. Actually, talking about suicide provides an opportunity to communicate about it. That's why we believe students appreciate our visits. Not everyone around them is willing to have this conversation. Suicide is what happens when people are out of options due to their circumstances, or they don't have the tools or resources to figure things out in life.

We imagine Ben was overwhelmed for various reasons, most unknown to us because knowing Ben, he wouldn't want to burden us with his struggles. I have come to understand that people with suicidal thoughts don't want to die, they just don't want to hurt anymore. I'm confident Ben's pain encompassed physical, mental, and emotional pain. Nobody likes to be in pain. Would you agree? Does this statement seem realistic? Relatable? Suicide happens when it appears there is no end in sight or alternative to the pain being felt. It tears me up to think that Benjamin felt such pain! Yet he hid it so well, like many people do.

Are you hiding pain? A smile on the outside does not always reflect true to what is being felt on the inside. Regardless of talent, looks, success, or wealth, people struggle! We all do! Struggles are part of life! It's just not the part people typically share. Instead of being *real,* many seek acceptance to find their worth through the *reel.* I've wished for the ability to see what others are actually feeling on the inside since each of us are really the only ones that know this truth about ourselves. Oh yes, we can project to everyone else how great our lives are or how we hope to portray them as and even convince ourselves they are great. And when we're being honest, that's wonderful! But I've learned over time and in many instances that these exterior displays or actions are deceiving. People seek their value in the opinions of others, when, in essence, we are the ones who have to live with ourselves and navigate through our failures and successes and are left to deal with all the emotions that accompany our circumstances. I love to celebrate the successes and blessings with others, but just as much, I appreciate those who have the strength to admit when they're struggling. It's important for us to understand that it's OK to not be OK! Not all the time or forever, obviously, but in the instances when we're feeling that way. And I ask, can you fathom what it would look like if we exposed our inside feelings to the external world just for a day? All the sadness, madness, hurts, pains, disappointments, feelings, and dire circumstances that we've pushed down in order to avoid dealing with and instead resort to coping mechanisms that offer temporary distractions but no permanent resolution.

Let's face it, there is a lot of yuck that needs our attention and forgiveness that needs to happen. As Pastor Rick Warren stated, "Real forgiveness is unconditional. There are no requirements attached to it. You don't earn it, you don't deserve it. Forgiveness is not based on a promise to never do it again. You offer forgiveness to somebody whether they ask for it or not. Also, forgiveness isn't minimizing the seriousness of the offense." I am confident Benjamin was hurt by others, disappointed in his circumstances, and felt alone at times. Unfortunately, my spiritual growth was immature and not in the place I am today where I could have suggested that Ben offer these wrongdoers forgiveness. And what does unforgiveness offer, may I ask? It offers distress and brings on insecurities, fears, stress, anxiety, and depression. It creates a place where the light in life is dimmed, and, unfortunately, it was where Ben was at. One of the statements he shared in his suicide letter was that he, "didn't see a light in the tunnel." My prayer is that you find it in your heart to forgive so you can see the light in the tunnel. Even if it's only a tiny flicker of light, there is still hope.

Whether you're a student we've reached to date, a student we will reach in the future, an adult, or anyone reading this book, I pray this for you:

Get rid of all bitterness, rage and anger, brawling and slander, along with
every form of malice. Be kind and compassionate to one another,
forgiving each other, just as in Christ God forgave you.
Ephesians 4:31-32 (NIV)

I also want to share my insight on relationships being a cause for suicides. I feel that I need to address the correlation between suicide and relationships, whether romantic or platonic. I've never done a formal assessment, but if somebody were to ask me, "With the survivors you've talked to, are the majority of suicides linked to a relationship?" my answer would be a resounding *yes*. While some suicides have been carried out by females, a majority of the suicides we have encountered have included males who were in a relationship that did not go as they had hoped for or expected. There have been many instances of people taking their lives by suicide who were in married relationships or dating relationships. It's heartbreaking to think of someone who has endured a marriage or has aspirations for a blooming relationship but gets thrown into the pit of "crummy" because of infidelity, a breakup, or whatever the circumstances might be, leaving someone in the relationship with a sense of brokenness.

Over and over again, I've heard survivors say to me, "I knew the person was hurting, but I didn't know to ask him/her if they were OK." I ask you, please, if you take anything away from reading this book, reach out to someone if you know they are hurting. It's OK to ask someone if they are OK. And I cannot stress enough, it's also OK not to be OK! If you're the one who is struggling, please be honest and ask for help! If you're the person who asks and learns that your loved one is struggling, please support their honesty and offer to assist in their search to find the help and support they need. It takes work, requires letting your guard down and putting your pride aside, but isn't your loved one's life worth it?

Don't make the assumption that they will survive whatever hurt they are going through. I made that mistake! When someone is hurting, that is when they need your support the most! You may not like or agree with the situation this person has gotten themselves into, but that doesn't matter. You can start by simply asking them, "How are you doing with all of this?" Now whether they will open up and are honest with you is something you cannot control. But at least you showed up and offered your support and let them know you care. Silence is deafening and sometimes disastrous for someone who is hurting. I urge you to be the person who breaks that silence by reaching out.

Another note of advice is if you do reach out and that person tells you they are "fine," don't assume it's the truth to make yourself feel better. Saying we're "OK" or "fine" is what we've been trained to say in our society, and it's also what we are trained to hear. Once we hear those words, we tend to quickly move on with our lives. Most people are not invested enough in someone to hear anything other than, "I'm fine," or, "I'm OK." Our society is not made up of cold-hearted people, but everyone is so busy, right? I mean, come on, we have a lot going on! If a person replies with, "I'm not OK. I'm having a hard time," do we really act upon it, or does it fall to the wayside? When I asked my son, "Ben, are you thinking of harming yourself?" his response to me was a soft, assuring, "No, Mom." And I believed him! *I heard exactly what I wanted to hear from Ben and without giving a second thought to the possibility that he wasn't being honest, silently let out a huge sigh of relief—until a week later when he killed himself!* I should have prodded more. We only know what we know, and this was a horrific, hard-learned, life-changing, heart-breaking lesson. Please learn from my experience! My advice is just because someone reassures you they won't harm themselves, it doesn't mean they won't! Have the courage to openly ask if they have a suicide plan. If they do, then go to them immediately or call 911.

Being invested in someone who is struggling takes effort and time. In our society, time is a luxury that we hold on to tightly and don't necessarily share freely with someone who isn't a family member or close friend. But this is *the* opportunity that we cannot step away from. If someone is hurting, struggling, or in crisis, we need to remind them they are not alone in their struggle. They have a whole world around them that is better because of their existence. People do care. People in crisis sometimes feel that the people around them don't care. It's become my mission to let anyone and everyone know that we do care. I've shared my phone number and email with countless people. I've had people in my home, taken them to church, invited them to support group meetings, invited them to family holidays, and spoken to them at all times, day and night. If I can help save one person from making the decision to take their life, then it's all worth it. And you might wish to consider as I'm sharing this is that the one person reaching out to me could be *your* person.

Terry and I had previously taken QPR (Question, Persuade, Refer) suicide prevention training in order to recognize the warning signs of suicide. We also accepted an invite from our friend in Kaukauna,

Barb, and completed the ASIST Suicide Prevention Training Program. Studies and government reports can be read on LivingWorks ASIST (www.livingworks.net). They show that this course improves trainee skills and readiness, is safe for trainees with no adverse effects, increases hope, and reduces suicidality. It has also been shown to increase general counseling and listening skills, and most importantly, it's saving lives. An important message I want to share is that suicide is not something that only a few of us need to know about. Suicide is a major issue that I hope and pray becomes one that society starts proactively speaking about.

Looking back at this training, it was apparent who had been impacted directly by suicide. The training included role-playing, and while others utilized the beneficial tools learned, Terry's approach was much more personal. Terry played out this role as if the person was Ben, and Terry was desperately trying to save him. We watched Terry's interactions with the "suicidal person" as he expressed how much he loved him and how sorry he was for the pain he was in and how he would miss him terribly if he died and how he wanted to help him through this challenging time he was experiencing. I felt as though Terry was praying for a second chance so our son could be spared from suicide. His participation was emotional for all who witnessed it. Some of the participants were moved to tears, and our instructors were speechless as they collected themselves before acknowledging Terry and proceeding with the training.

As neighbors, teachers, clergy members, community members, and innocent strangers, when we see someone needing help, we must have the courage to say something. The slogan, "If you see something, say something," came about after the national tragedy of 9/11. I challenge you to use this same philosophy when you see someone in crisis. They might not be a danger to others, but they could certainly be a danger to themselves. So *say something*! We all have communities where someone should be able to receive some support. I define communities as circles or groups we interact with, whether it's within a family, church, school, college, sports team, hobby club, online group, or at work. We may encounter signs of crisis in person, over the phone, in a text, in an email, or in a social media posting. Don't let those calls for help go unanswered, and don't be embarrassed because of them.

I recently had a conversation with a parent whose child was struggling. From what was shared, I was very concerned and encouraged the parents to be vigilant as I responded to the conversations, comments, and other insights we discussed during our time together. What hurt my heart was when the parent said, "We don't want anyone to know about this." That's *so* unfortunate! That's the stigma of mental health! This needs to stop. I explained my feelings to the father, stating that if his son had cancer, I imagined he would be willing to share that news with others and receive the support needed as they worked through that. Mental health is a health issue!

Here's where the BENS Hope mantra comes in. *You are not alone.* From the moment Ben took his life, we were walking a devastating journey. We want to help you. Let's walk together. As hard as it is to do this, it's part of the healing process.

I have to share a more recent journal entry as proof that I'm still—and always will be—in the healing process.

3/8/2022

Carrie called me today to let me know she took Desi on her first outing to a library. I shared with her that I'd been crying about this book and getting ready for tonight's SOS meeting. She said, "I want you to know, Mom, that you did a great job raising us. Even a great job raising Ben."

I look back at those breakups Ben had and how he didn't know what to do with himself, and I think about how I felt back then as I told him, "Gee, stop acting so crazy about this." But I didn't know how he was feeling, and I didn't ask him how he was REALLY feeling. I didn't get invested enough in his pain and struggle. Things that I shoulda, coulda, woulda done. I don't get another chance to do them with Ben. But if somehow, some way, our loss can open the eyes of others and offer insight, help, and hope, that's what GOD wants us to do. I know that to be true, and I'm just going to have to keep hanging on to that. Admittedly, sometimes I don't, and it's so agonizing and painful. I asked a medium one time, "Why didn't I get the intuition that Ben was going to take his life?" The medium replied, "You weren't supposed to." As for myself, I've always had intuition, a feeling, a vibe. But that day, I didn't get one. I've come to terms with the fact that it happened the way Ben wanted it to, and I've concluded that God knew from the beginning that suicide would touch our lives in the way it has. Ben, like each of us, had free will; Ben made the decision, God allowed it to happen, but God did not cause it. This is our journey as it was destined to be. I don't have to like it, and trust me, I do not, but I continue working through this reality every single day of my life. I'm reminded to find goodness because there are still so many blessings. I love knowing that I have my sight to see, my loved ones close, and I can enjoy the beauty in sunrises, sunsets, rainbows, and waterfalls. And then there are the views on the lake from the boathouse we visit each year. Wow!

My heart has definitely felt the worst of pain, but this same heart has also felt tremendous love before Ben's suicide and, I might add, even JOY after it, something I never thought possible following Ben's suicide. I give thanks for my sense of hearing. Imagine the delight I feel when I hear the sounds of my family's voices during our visits, whether in person or through social media. How about the wonderful smiles and giggles coming from our beautiful grandbaby, Desiree...priceless! Or waking up to the birds in the stillness of the morning before the sunrise. The fact that oxygen is available to keep us breathing should not go unnoticed every waking moment of our day. While I no longer drink coffee, I recall the excitement of being with Norma and having my daily first cup, mmm! Or the taste of ice cream from Grab a Cone or chocolates from Betty Jane Candies, so delightful! And what about the sense of touch? I've held many hands and offered and received many hugs. I love hugs; it's a gift where in giving, you receive! I love hugs! My point here is that while I could sit in a chair in a dark room all day and be sad about my circumstances, I've made the intentional decision to find goodness in each day. I practice gratitude daily and not just necessarily during the morning or night but throughout the day. I'm in constant communication with God, thanking Him for my blessings because there are so many. I also know that God can use tragic events to bring goodness because He proclaimed this to me.

This definitely takes me back to the night of Ben's suicide. That night, we couldn't get ahold of Ben. I started to get anxious. I decided to call his roommate, Caleb. On speaker phone, we listened as Caleb entered Ben's room and cried out, "NO, NO, NO, NO, THIS ISN'T HAPPENING." Terry was beside me, yelling back to Caleb, "Call 911! Call 911!" Even though we received a call from the coroner ahead of our departure informing us that our son was deceased, Terry remained in denial, desperate to get to Benjamin so he could receive the help he needed. I didn't have the capacity to say more to Terry to convince him otherwise. I was in shock and dealing with hyperventilation, hoping to stay conscious. As I made a call to my boss en route, I didn't recognize my own voice. My throat was restricted; I wasn't sure what was happening at the time, but I do recall sounding like Kermit the Frog. I'm not sure how many things were going on in my body and mind, but there were multiple things happening. Our two-and-a-half-hour drive was excruciating and the longest ride of our lives! We were in disbelief, desperately wanting to wake up from this horrifying nightmare.

Terry, Mom, and I arrived first and met up with Mandy, Carrie, and Matt, who joined us at Ben's. What a scene. There were police lights and officials everywhere. I just wanted to see Ben, but that wouldn't happen for a while. We were ushered into the house and directed by the officials to the chief medical examiner, Tim Candahl. Amidst this nightmare, Mr. Candahl was kind and compassionate of our circumstances. I recall him talking about Ben's corneas being donated and us having to call the Department of Health regarding Ben's tissue and organ donations. He talked about us going to the police department in the morning to retrieve Ben's belongings—his gun, computer, cell phone, etc. He shared hotels we could stay at overnight. I clung to his every word, still trying to make sense of where I was and if this was really happening or if I was stuck in a bad nightmare. Finally, after what seemed like an eternity, we were given permission to go see Ben.

And so, we made our way back into his bedroom. My mind was going in a million directions, still trying to process this reality. I remember the hallway seemed to be longer than it was on our last visit. Ben and Caleb hadn't been in this place long. They had recently moved from La Crosse to Onalaska to accommodate a third roommate, Travis, who also worked at Kaplan. As I walked into Ben's room, there lay our wonderful son Benjamin on the floor, wrapped in his bed comforter with only his face exposed. As I lay across my deceased son, hysterical and crying inconsolably, I ran my hands through Ben's hair, kissing his forehead and repeating, "I'm so sorry, Ben, I didn't know." My heart broke for being unaware he was hurting so badly that he desired to end his life. I apologized for missing the signs and not knowing the depth of his pain. It was agonizing.

I must share that reading through this manuscript about Ben's suicide takes my breath away, even years later. I literally went back in time to that dreadful night and wept tears as I did that night, still in shock that Ben's suicide *is* my/our reality. As I wept and watched tears fall onto my glasses, I knew I had to share with those of you struggling that *you do matter,* and that if you weren't here, your loved ones would miss you tremendously. Suicide is optional. It does not have to happen. There are resources to help you through this season in your life. I cannot stress enough that suicide is a permanent solution to a temporary situation. Things can and will get better, even if not in this moment, even if not in the time you desire. But I promise they will.

Yes, I know, life is not fair. People can be mean. People can mess with your feelings. People will walk over you and kick you to the side. I am sorry. Have you heard that hurt people hurt people? Is it just me, or has anyone else noticed that there are a lot of hurting people in our world? That is why terrible things happen. I know you might think people don't understand what you're feeling, and you're probably right because there's only one you, and only you know exactly how you're feeling. You're unique; you're one of a kind. That's how God wired you! You're a masterpiece of His; you were chosen and part of His plan. Please know that people do care. Please reach out for help. We don't know if you're in a place so dark you can't feel the light. We don't know if you're masking your troubled soul. We do know we don't want you to leave the stage in the middle of your song, like it references in Rascal Flatts's song "Why."

※

Let not your hearts be troubled, neither let them be afraid.
John 14:27b (ESV)

※

In Him (God) we were also chosen, having been predestined
according to the plan of Him who works out everything
in conformity with the purpose of His will.
Ephesians 1:11 (NIV)

As we return to the night of Ben's suicide, I realize this might be a lot for some of you to process. But it's my story and part of my journey, and I know there are others of you reading this who can also relate because suicide has impacted your journey. The night it happened changed our lives forever. As I cried hysterically while lying over my deceased son, something extraordinary happened, and it's important to share because it's been a factor in what has kept me here at times I contemplated leaving. Suddenly, this calming sensation swept over me, and I looked up from Benjamin to see Terry, Mandy, Carrie, Matt, and my mom standing above me. As I did, these words flowed from my mouth: "We will find goodness in this." I knew the words proclaimed did not come from this inconsolable mom who just lost her son. I know this sacred experience was a divine intervention.

At the funeral, I found myself consoling countless mourners who asked, "How could this happen to you?" or "How could this happen to your family?" My response was always the same: "God needed someone strong, and He knew we could do this." Again, I was bewildered as I proclaimed words from my mouth that were not my own.

And the peace of God, which transcends all understanding,
will guard your hearts and your minds in Christ Jesus.
Philippians 4:7 (NIV)

He will wipe away every tear from their eyes, and death shall be no more,
neither shall there be mourning, nor crying, nor pain anymore,
for the former things have passed away.
Revelation 21:4 (ESV)

CHAPTER 12

MY JOURNEY TO BEING A GRIEF, GRACE, AND GRATITUDE SPECIALIST

But he said to me, "My grace is sufficient for you, for my power is made perfect in weakness." Therefore I will boast all the more gladly about my weaknesses, so that Christ's power may rest on me.
2 Corinthians 12:9 (NIV)

Experiencing grief, asking for grace, and practicing gratitude has become my ministry. Their significance and meaning have transformed consistently alongside my circumstances in life. What an enlightening journey it has been! It is a lifetime of learning, and while I certainly don't have everything figured out by any means, I am confident in the direction God is leading me and am humbled to serve in the capacity He chooses to help others.

Religion, faith, and spirituality have definitely accompanied me on my life's journey. I am confident that while reading this book you have witnessed my spiritual pilgrimage evolving. At the age of nineteen, I became very inquisitive about what happens after we die. My curiosity spiked after losing my little brother, Greg. I often reflect on that Friday night. I was still at work and recall hearing sirens wailing as an ambulance sped by the bank. Little did I know it was en route to aid in a tragedy that would impact our family.

After I got off of work, Terry and I spent time with some friends before heading to the bowling alley to meet my dad, my brother, Al, and others in the bowling league. It was well after start time, and Dad and Al weren't there yet; it was apparent something had happened. Cell phones were not made widely available in 1981, so we waited anxiously. When Dad finally arrived, it was immediately apparent that something was wrong. My eyes moved from the disheveled look on Dad's face to the knees of his jeans, soiled with dirt stains. He slowly approached us, explaining there had been an accident and that we needed to get to the hospital.

It was late as we climbed into Sheriff Hottenstein's vehicle and made our way across town through the dreary rain on that dark night. Dad never once mentioned Greg's name even though I asked about him repeatedly. When we finally arrived at the hospital, I leaped out of the car, bolted through the emergency entrance, and ran frantically down the corridor. My heart was racing and my head pounding as an enormous lump pulsated in my throat. As we were ushered into a hallway, there lay my older brother, Al, also injured in the accident, on a gurney awaiting transport to a hospital in Iowa. As we entered a doorway into a room, I expected to see Greg, but instead there stood Mom, alone, waiting for us. As I glanced around the room, I asked Mom where Greg was. Her eyes looked downwards as she replied through tears that Greg was gone. "Gone where?" I asked, thinking he'd been transported to another hospital. Then Mom proclaimed words I'll never forget: "We lost him." LOST HIM?! What the hell did she mean by that?! Her words meant that Greg was gone—as in dead.

When Father Bud, our priest from St Mary's Church, arrived, we were all still in shock. I had calmed down after my initial ballistic reaction of breaking a chair after learning this horrible news. The first question I asked Father Bud was, "Is heaven real?" Of course I had heard people speak of heaven, but never did it mean more to me than in this moment! I needed to know! Is there more to dying than death itself, or is that it? We stay here until our number is up then lights out and it's all over?! Father Bud's response was a resounding, "Yes, heaven is real!" He explained the beauty that awaits us in heaven and reassured us Greg was there with our grandparents and other loved ones who've gone before as well as the angels and our Heavenly Father. I found comfort then and am still aware of God's dwelling place that offers peace, love, community, and worship. This wonder is available to all who believe in God. Years later when I finally picked up a Bible, I found scripture to validate this truth.

Your dead shall live; their bodies shall rise. You who dwell in the
dust, awake and sing for joy! For your dew is a dew of
light, and the earth will give birth to the dead.
Isaiah 26:19 (ESV)

But our citizenship is in heaven. And we eagerly await a Savior
from there, the Lord Jesus Christ, who, by the power that enables
Him to bring everything under His control, will transform
our lowly bodies so that they will be like His glorious body.
Philippians 3:20-21 (NIV)

After that, we who are still alive and are left will be caught up
together with them in the clouds to meet the Lord in the air.
And so we will be with the Lord forever.
1 Thessalonians 4:17 (NIV)

My Father's house has many rooms; if that were not so, would I
have told you that I am going there to prepare a place for you?
And if I go and prepare a place for you, I will come back and
take you to be with me that you also may be where I am.
You know the way to the place where I am going.
John 14:2-4 (NIV)

As I shared earlier, Greg's death was not our first family loss; there have been others, but Greg's was the first loss of one of my "persons." I identify my persons as the ones I love with every ounce of my being and would do anything for! They're the ones who mean the world to me. It's hard to understand the pain and depth that accompanies a loss unless you've experienced it, especially the loss of one of your persons. But, like everything else, we only know what we know, right?

Whether losing your person in death, divorce, a friendship, a relationship, or otherwise, loss takes you on a journey like you've never known before. It's an experience you question whether you'll survive. Some moments you feel like you're going to get through it, and in the very next moment, you are caught up in excruciating pain, feeling you cannot go on. Honestly, when the loss is your person, you may have moments you don't wish to go on, or, at least, I felt that way. The unbearable pain of losing Benjamin has been the most arduous challenge in my life. I cannot tell you the number of times I initially contemplated checking out. I share this because it may resonate with some of you who are currently feeling agonizing pain from losing your person. From my own experience, I'm grateful God's given me the strength and desire to stay here because there are so many things I would have missed out on otherwise! And it saddens me profusely not having Benjamin here to enjoy the blessings that awaited him. I know with confidence he would have adored Desi and Olive. I can envision his "Ben Face" just thinking about it.

If you can relate to losing your person, my heart goes out to you. If you have yet to experience the loss of your person, please know it is possible to survive even on the days you don't think you can carry on. I have prayed and cried my way through horrific losses on multiple occasions and can promise you it is possible to survive the unthinkable. I am proof of this. If you're struggling with loss, I am sending so much love and so many hugs to you at this very moment and am asking God to wrap you in His unconditional and everlasting love.

Here is a scripture verse that brought me comfort that I'd like to share. I pray it offers you comfort as well.

Then Jesus said, "Come to me, all of you who are weary and
carry heavy burdens, and I will give you rest."
Matthew 11:28 (NLT)

Please give yourself the grace to grieve in any way or shape that works for you. While others may not understand or offer empathy toward your loss, each individual's loss is their own to process and work through. We just have to remember to keep moving forward and not get stuck in our grief. And I encourage you to talk about your person. They're an important part of your life and shall never be forgotten. It's allowing ourselves to deal and feel that offers the healing we wish for as we move forward on our grief and healing journey. Also, be intentional about taking time and doing something special just for you. This isn't being selfish if it's something that brings you joy and keeps you centered. I've found sanctity, peace, and grace through practicing self-care.

Working through my grief, I desperately sought ways to find peace and comfort. Honestly, I wondered if it was even possible to recover from this horrific loss. I recall all those times it felt impossible initially, but I'm still here, folks, and that speaks volumes. Here are some of the things I'd like to share that I did to help me through my traumatizing grief:

Cry

Breathe

Get out of bed every day

Shower

Eat

Get sleep/nap

Allow yourself to be vulnerable

Reflect on what will never be

Reflect on what is

Listen to others struggling

Share your story

Let the tears flow freely

Deal with the pain instead of avoiding it

Don't worry about what others think

Be kind to yourself

Enjoy the happy, silly moments

Attended grief support classes

Seek professional counseling—if it doesn't work, seek another counselor

Ask your employer if they have an Employee Assistance Program (EAP)

Attend a religious outreach program

Practice spiritual exploration

Read related books

Read the Bible

Go see a movie

Watch the TV show Dancing with the Stars or dance

Cry, cry, and cry some more

Pray a lot

Drink

Exercise

Go for a walk outside

Get on the treadmill—even if you have to use your armpits to hold yourself up

Massage therapy

Acupuncture

Reiki

Reflexology

Essential oils

Write in a journal

In addition, I:

Accepted invitations to speak to groups/organizations in and outside the community

Shared my story to educate others

Shared my stoy and offered SOS support to others in and outside our community

Shared my story and helped others with SOS support on campus at UW-Platteville

Rode my bike

Cuddled with our grandpuppy, Olive

Listened to Family Life Radio daily

Some of these techniques might be of interest to you while others may not. Either way, that's OK. We each have our own journey, and our grief experience is as unique as the person we loved, lost, and mourned. This was validated during a grief and loss course I took at UW-Madison while obtaining a certificate to become a grief support specialist. When my coach, Tammy, suggested I take a grief counseling certification course, I agreed immediately. Registration was due that week, so there was no time to talk myself out of enrolling. I was initially intimidated by this sophisticated group. The majority of them were well traveled, bilingual, and held master's and doctorate degrees. I was curious what this hometown girl who married her high school sweetheart could offer. It became clear that others desired to learn about my grief experiences, survival, and how I moved forward. For me, I've learned that there is no getting over Ben's death, but rather, I am incorporating his death into my life and finding what that looks like as I continue on my journey.

Mind you, Ben's death was not like any loss I'd ever experienced before. Ben was not only my person, Ben was my child! I brought him into this world with a lifetime of dreams and aspirations ahead. Never would I have expected any of my children to leave this world before me, but this parents' worst nightmare became our reality with Ben's suicide. Here I always thought the greatest pain my kids would ever cause me in this lifetime was that of what I experienced in childbirth, but that was before I had to bury my son. The pain of childbirth went away, while the pain of burying my child is ingrained in me forever. For those of you who can relate to this reality, I am sending love, prayers, and hugs to you. The only thing I can imagine worse than losing a child is having a child estranged to you due to addiction, unforgiveness, misunderstandings, mental health struggles and disorders, abuse, neglect, lack of support, gender identity, religion, political views, or whatever is causing the despair. Again, I send love, hugs, and prayers to you, asking God to bring reconciliation.

Religion was part of our upbringing. It was something our parents passed on to us from their upbringing and expected us to practice. The beliefs that accompany religion meant us attending church every Sunday and on the holy days of obligation, partaking in catechism classes on Wednesday evenings, and making the required sacraments of the Catholic Church. Terry and I got married in the Catholic Church and raised our children accordingly. This was the extent of our knowledge on religion; it was not good, bad, right, or wrong, it's just what we knew based on what we were shown and had experienced. We are grateful to our parents for introducing us to Jesus, the chief cornerstone of our faith.

Later on my journey, I became interested in spirituality and even found my way into New Age practices, including mediumship. My soul sister and dear friend, Barb, and I started attending weekly evening classes that were offered locally. Some memorable experiences included guided meditations, journaling, channeling spirits, connecting with spirit guides via readings, and so on. It was intriguing, and we couldn't get enough until I did and realized these sessions had served in the capacity needed. It was time to move on to the next chapter, but questions still lingered.

Little did I know this next chapter would involve Katie, who I met at those classes. She was beautiful inside and out and had the gift of channeling. It was incredible to witness what Katie's clairvoyant gift offered to others. To learn more, I started hosting Katie in my home, inviting guests to join us.

Katie, who lived about thirty minutes away, typically met one-on-one with interested prospects in my home. To prepare the house, I would burn sage, light candles, have background music playing, and dim the lights ahead of Katie's arrival. Soon after, our guest was welcomed and given a few minutes to relax before being ushered downstairs to the aroma of essential oils to meet Katie. After introductions, Katie offered a blessing ahead of the reading. I took notes as Katie shared messages with our guests who awaited eagerly to get answers and validation from their deceased loved ones. This chapter was short-lived, as Katie moved away. Questions remained in my heart as I continued seeking and searching, moving into the next chapter of life.

Who would have known that my connection to Katie would lead me in a new direction? It was Katie who introduced me to Ava, and I had the opportunity to study mediumship with her. I felt confident working with Ava since she was a reverend. She offered me comfort as I proceeded on my spiritual journey. Even though attending her classes meant late-evening travels, this opportunity excited me. What an extraordinary experience it was! Sharing insight with others offered comfort and confirmation. It was incredible to witness! I felt blessed in these moments and thankful to have Ava as my teacher. Still, questions lingered.

An opportunity came up to see Katie again. I was hosting a bridal shower in my home and asked Katie to share her gift with our guests, which she agreed to. I did notice some guests elected to stay upstairs while Katie spoke to the others downstairs. I imagined they had reasoning for their reservations. After sharing insight with the bride-to-be and other guests in attendance, Katie turned to me and my sister, saying there would be a big event coming up around the holidays that would bring us even closer together. We wondered what this event might be.

Little did we know then that the big event Katie referred to would occur November 11, 2014: the day Ben took his life. Little did I know then that Ava would be the one to offer prayers at Ben's wake.

I know these experiences happened because they were supposed to, including meeting these people on my journey. I appreciate the blessings that came out of it and the valuable lessons I learned from it. But I also know that it was Ben's death that brought me back to my faith in Christianity. God knew the route that needed to be taken in order for me to find what I was actually seeking: a relationship with the Divine Source, the One who has the answers to our questions and prayers. For me, God is this source and has been my saving grace ever since. I've learned not to expect anyone to provide what is only available from God.

Now faith is confidence in what we hope for and
assurance about what we do not see.
Hebrews 11:1 (NIV)

I will instruct you and teach you in the way you should go;
I will counsel you with my loving eye on you.
Psalm 32:8 (NIV)

It may or may not come as a surprise to you, but I never picked up a Bible before Ben's death! Well, I'll take that back. I did pick up a Bible on a few occasions, which typically happened during my travels and hotel stays with Terry. I'd move the Bible out of the way to get to the phone book. I needed the phone book, specifically the yellow pages, that provided a listing of businesses by category to find recommended places to wine and dine or attractions to visit. While I didn't previously read the Bible, I have been reading it since Ben's passing. I know what some of you might be saying because I am confident I've said something similar. I mean, we only know what we know, right? But I can share that I do have a new appreciation for why it's called the Living Word— it speaks! Previously, I questioned what could be relevant in today's world from a Bible dating back to Jesus over 2000 years ago, but there's more than I ever imagined! There are lessons that offer insight and direction with all that's happening today in our modern world. The Bible shares the hardships of others and how they persevered through them. Struggles are not new; they have been going on for centuries. In these challenges, we dig deep and tap into unknown strength within ourselves that we previously didn't know existed. It's a gift from God and the Holy Spirit.

For those who have difficulty understanding the Bible, I get it; I've been there too. But rest assured, there are many resources and commentaries that help explain the Bible in layman terms. If you prefer watching TV, I encourage you to check out *The Chosen*, a television series created, directed, and co-written by Dallas Jenkins and starring Jonathan Roumie, who portrays Jesus. It depicts the people who met and followed Jesus—regular folks, just like us. It is powerful! And if you question watching *The Chosen*, I encourage you to at least check out the documentary *Unfiltered: Gen Z Reacts to The Chosen*. The faith and religion of the diverse participants who participated in this viewing were not identified. However, watching *The Chosen*, they found themselves relating to the characters as well as experiences we're all familiar with, such as rejection, alienation, and mental health, to name a few. And most importantly, they witnessed how Jesus loves each and every one of us, regardless of the wrong decisions or poor choices we've made or our lack of desire to know Him. From watching *The Chosen*, these participants found themselves opening up, being vulnerable, and sharing their stories, tears, and all. Jesus offers love, compassion, and acceptance, and isn't that what we're looking for? Christianity doesn't say to close your eyes and believe but rather to check it out for yourself. Your opinion of Jesus is a matter of choosing death, not only in this life but in the life to come.

Ask and it will be given to you; seek and you will find; knock and the
door will be opened to you. For everyone who asks receives; the one
who seeks finds; and to the one who knocks, the door will be opened.
Matthew 7:7-8 (NIV)

Each of these personal discoveries of religion, faith, and spirituality
prepared me for the next chapter in my life. Through presentations
and speaking engagements, I have a better understanding of why God
put me on this earth and the path ahead of me. I have appreciation for
what I have learned through my experiences and clarity on what my
purpose in life is supposed to be. God has guided and provided me with
hope since the very night Ben died so I can serve in this capacity.

"For I know the plans I have for you," declares the Lord, "plans to prosper
you and not to harm you, plans to give you hope and a future."
Jeremiah 29:11

I am also thankful for the signs that God has given to me, as well
as Terry, so we can fulfill our mission through BENS Hope. We are
humbled and honored to serve in this capacity that has such significant
meaning.

But in your hearts revere Christ as Lord. Always be prepared to give an
answer to everyone who asks you to give the reason for the hope
that you have. But do this with gentleness and respect.
1 Peter 3:15 (NIV)

Supporting bereaved people, I will share that grief doesn't advise of
its appearance ahead of time like we're accustomed to when we RSVP
to an invitation. It rears its head unexpectedly any time it desires, and
in some instances, surprises us in the most staggering ways when

we least expect it. I encourage you to offer yourself grace, and rather than trying to avoid this unwanted intrusion, manage the feelings presented in the way that works best for you. Options may include openly sharing, stepping away for a moment to collect yourself, or taking some time to be alone.

Grieving can be triggered by unexpected events and simple things you'd never expect. I was caught off guard when my daughters asked during one of our Christmas seasons if they could take their respective ornaments home to use on their Christmas trees. Since they both have their own places, of course this made sense in my mind but painfully, not in my heart. I retreated to the bathroom downstairs as tears exploded from my eyes. What was happening?! I didn't understand my reaction initially, but then it came to me. It wasn't about the girls taking their ornaments home. It was the realization that Ben's ornaments would never go home with him but remain with us because Ben isn't here; he'll never have his own Christmas tree or spend another Christmas with us. He is gone forever. Once I stepped away and had time to process my feelings, I came back to my family and tearfully shared the reasoning for my reaction. The girls eventually took their ornaments home, but it took me time to accept this, which is OK. Remember friends, it's OK not to be OK, and this is one of the many instances of me not being OK.

Another experience came when both Mandy and Carrie surpassed Benjamin's age of 27, his age at his death. They were both officially "older" than Ben. I cried out to God again, expressing my sorrow. I always shared that Ben was our oldest, and now this statement was no longer true. As I wept, God spoke, gently reminding me that Ben will always be my firstborn. This realization immediately brought my heart peace and comfort. Leave it to God! If you're seeking answers, I encourage you to talk it over with God and listen for answers. His grace dwelling within you can be the greatest gift of peace you may ever find.

My early retirement came at God's request. It took a long time, but I eventually came to the realization that working at the bank had served its purpose. As difficult of a decision as it was to leave, it was time to move forward to the next chapter. Thank goodness God is patient. I am tremendously thankful for my tenure at Mound City Bank. Holding the position of internal auditor and writing countless audit reports enhanced my ability to write *Tears of Love*. These last years have offered me much, but honestly, if you asked me what my greatest takeaway has been, I would say the most valuable lesson over these past years was God teaching me the fruit of the Spirit. I've had countless opportunities to learn and grow in kindness, goodness, gentleness, love, faithfulness, joy, peace, patience, and self-control, both at work and in life. Of course, I'm still a work in progress and always will be. I pray to become my best self: the person God created me to be.

But the fruit of the Spirit is love, joy, peace, patience, kindness, goodness, faithfulness, gentleness, self-control; against such things there is no law.
Galatians 5:22-23 (ESV)

As God was nudging me to retire early and write this book, Terry and I were busy with fulfilling obligations for BENS Hope. It was a juggling act between working full time, completing requests for BENS Hope, fulfilling my weekly commitments, and ensuring progress of the audit schedule appeased the BOD at each quarterly meeting, many times loyally working ten- to twelve-hour days to ensure I did so. I didn't realize how busy we were with BENS Hope until my editor, Rebecca, inquired. For the benefit of this book, she asked me to provide the number of BENS-Hope-related presentations Terry and I have made. While not all-inclusive, it appears we have represented BENS Hope at approximately 300 events to date, reaching thousands of people. It is truly amazing to see how and where God is using us through Ben's story and BENS Hope.

Some of you may be questioning how I hear from God. Well, whether taking time to read from the Bible, hearing a message through a song, or sitting silently, you too can have this experience. Our BENS Hope nonprofit, this book, and the agenda for school presentations were all God's ideas. Hopefully there's been enough evidence in this book for you to realize this is not of our own will. I mean, if it weren't for God, I would have checked out, friends. But He has a purpose for me, for you, and for each of us! I pray you take time to listen to what He's calling you to do.

God also gifted me with a new title for my future work. I still recall the morning I was staying at Mandy's home when God woke me from my sleep. As I heard Him whisper it, goosebumps traveled all over my entire body. God told me that in my service to helping others, I will be a grief, grace and gratitude specialist. I was initially really excited about it until I thought, "Wait! How am I a specialist?" Then God reminded me of the extremely intense training I'd been through in life and how these horrific experiences were preparing me. As for grace, God wants us to grow strong in giving grace to others and offering forgiveness unconditionally. I get it, it is easier said than done. But we know who actually pays for unforgiveness. You.

But by the grace of God I am what I am, and His grace toward me was
not in vain. On the contrary, I worked harder than any of them,
though it was not I, but the grace of God that is with me.
1 Corinthians 15:10 (ESV)

Terry and I became very intentional about practicing gratitude on a nightly basis. Amidst the hardships we encounter, taking time to reflect on the goodness each day brings serves as a wonderful reminder of how blessed we truly are.

Rejoice always, pray without ceasing, give thanks in all circumstances;
for this is the will of God in Christ Jesus for you.
1 Thessalonians 5:16-18 (ESV)

BENS Hope is a mission Terry and I have taken on together. We strive toward bringing hope and offering kindness to others. It's because of the misfortune of Ben's suicide that I've found my ministry and my purpose and accepted the vision God has put on my heart. My approach to serving others is a faith-based approach since that's what kept me here and has gotten me through the challenges in life that I have faced. Becoming a grief, grace and gratitude specialist will be a blessing to others but also to me as I serve in this ministry that is truly heart led.

I wish to reassure you that it is possible to find goodness in horrific circumstances, my friends, but we have to put in the work to make this happen. Nobody else can do this work. Are you up for the challenge? I hope so.

Pastor Mark made a statement during his sermon December 26, 2021, and it stuck with me, and I feel it's worth repeating. He said, "We all have a theology of God based on our circumstances, and these circumstances reorganize and reshape us and our lives." Thank you, Pastor Mark. Our circumstances have definitely reshaped us and our lives. Look how God elected to use our personal tragedy to impact and bless others.

CHAPTER 13

GODWINK REVELATIONS

The Lord is my strength and my shield; my heart trusts in Him, and He
helps me. My heart leaps for joy, and with my song I praise Him.
Psalm 28:7 (NIV)

Another thing that I have experienced since losing loved ones is what I refer to as a Godwink. It can be a sign that coincides with a deceased person's upcoming birthday, Angelversary, or sometimes just because. What I can share is that these Godwinks are honestly what have helped propel me forward in life. I feel like it's God's way of blessing me until I am reunited with my deceased loved ones.

Some question the reason why I see or hear things they might overlook or pay no attention to. Maybe it's because I believe in God and His Son, Jesus. Even though I don't understand the mystery of it all and continue learning every day, the one thing I am sure of is that *I believe.*

But blessed are your eyes because they see,
and your ears because they hear.
Matthew 13:16 (NIV)

Since Ben's passing, Terry, our daughters, and I have encountered Godwinks placed in our paths that I feel were surely put there by God,

Ben, or both! How that works exactly is unbeknownst to me. Since I've shared Godwink experiences with others, they have had their own experiences. Godwinks bring encouragement to my mission and hopefully curiosity of God to those listening so they can hopefully experience their own Godwinks. And it's not just that these signs show up, it's also about their impeccable timing, and sometimes, at crucial moments, that could be the difference between life and death!

So, let me provide you with additional examples of what I classify as Godwinks. Earlier in the book, I shared that during our school presentations we play a video by Rascal Flatts. While Terry and I always received divine guidance for our presentations, one question remained: how would we transition from the initial ice-breaker, the chicken dance, to the serious topic of suicide? Well, as God would have it, and, interestingly enough, one day one of my coworkers came running into my office. She knew of my belief in Godwinks and wanted to share what she'd just experienced. As she was getting ready for work that morning, she was looking for a white T-shirt to wear under her cardigan. She said she grabbed a random white T-shirt that happened to be from our BENS Hope annual 5K/2M Suicide Awareness/Prevention event. As she drove from her country home into town while listening to the radio, she realized the song "Why" by Rascal Flatts was playing, a song relevant to suicide. This definitely got her attention! As she drove on, she noticed something in the road ahead, and, as she got closer, she witnessed something she'd never seen previously in all her travels to work. As she neared the object, she witnessed an eagle take flight right before her eyes. Her mouth dropped open in awe! Sarah wasn't sure what all this meant, but she knew it meant something, and she had to share this with me. I am so grateful that Sarah didn't miss this Godwink. Since that time, "Why" has been used to set the stage for our school presentations. Thank you, Sarah, thank you, Rascal Flatts, and thank you, God, for another Godwink!

Here are additional Godwinks from my journal entries:

11/9/2016

Terry and I packed up and headed to Door County for a few days to relax and reflect before the two-year anniversary, or "Angelversary," of Ben's death. On our way out of town, we bought a rose and took it to Ben's grave, always a heartbreaking stop. Our drive to Door County proved to be one filled with Godwinks and reassurance that Ben is still with us in a new way. We witnessed prisms in the sky our entire way and angelic clouds that seemed to follow us. It was incredible and gave us a sense of comfort and love that was much needed. Our actual stay in Door County was like our lives these past two years: a roller coaster of emotions, happy moments, sadness, anger, tears, and laughter. But as time has gone on, the apologies between Terry and me have started to come sooner, and the love and support we share has become stronger.

9/15/2017

Arrived home after my appointment at Harmony House. As I pulled in the driveway, Terry was visiting with a young boy on his bike. I asked who he was talking to. He replied with such enthusiasm: "Greg." While my brother Greg was killed at fourteen years old, God sent his look-alike right to our front yard!

Saturday at work Carrie was informed that two new coworkers had started. She shared this with me on Sunday. "Guess what their names are?" she asked. Immediately, I guessed, "Ben." She said, "Yep, that's one of their names, guess what the other one's name is?" It didn't take long for her to reply. "Cullen," she stated. WOW! You can't make this stuff up! God is so good!

November 2019

Kari, my coworker and friend, recently lost her twenty-four-year-old friend, Levi, in an accident. After attending a funeral Saturday morning, she went home to get her two young sons. She said she just wanted to do something special because she was feeling so sad. On their way to get *pizza, she thought about our conversations of Godwinks and asked God to please give her a sign to let her know Levi was OK. While waiting for her pizza, an employee called out, "Pizza is ready for LEVI!" Come on, you can't make this stuff up!*

11/7/2019

Terry sent a text this morning saying he just got into his work truck and "Come as You Are" was playing. That song is always a hello from heaven: a "Hi" from Ben. I had just finished writing my work performance evaluation that included a note of thanks to my boss and workplace for supporting BENS Hope. After turning it in, "Come as You Are" was playing on the radio. Hi, Ben!

11/9/2019

My neighbor stopped by the weekend of Ben's five-year Angelversary. She came to me in the kitchen and said, "I have to tell you about an experience I had; what do you call those things?" "Godwinks?" I curiously replied. You have to understand that this was a big deal; she is not sold on being a believer. She told us her uncle had passed away this past week. While she was standing at the cemetery for her uncle's burial, she gazed in a certain direction and noticed the date on a random headstone. It was her mom's birth and death date. Then she looked in the opposite direction at another random headstone and saw her dad's birth and death date. That got her attention! She could not believe what just happened. She said to me, "There is some greater being out there." Folks, this is how Jesus gets our attention!

November 2019

I recall when Terry and I went to a school presentation in Mount Horeb. I was so nervous, anxious, and almost physically ill. I can never predict how we will be received when we arrive for these speaking events. When we pulled into the school parking lot, we found an empty stall, and right next to it was a blue Honda—the same kind of car Ben drove. That was the blessing I needed in that exact moment to know Ben was with us, and what a blessing it was to have that reassurance from God through this Godwink!

Christmas 2019

I am thankful for the blessings of Godwinks before and after Christmas. Terry and I went Christmas shopping the Sunday after Christmas to pick up gifts for Pam and Bruce, my sister and brother-in-law. We went to a shop in Mineral Point that had many images of cardinals with phrases saying that cardinals represent a loved one visiting from heaven. As we were walking to our vehicle, something caught my eye. I looked down to find a dime. This is always a hello sign from Benjamin since Terry, the girls, and I started finding dimes shortly after he died.

As I picked up the dime, I mentioned to Terry that others may wonder why anyone would be so excited about finding a dime. But we know what this represents, and that's what matters. When we got home, Terry noticed a cardinal in the bird feeder outside our kitchen window. How fitting for the morning we experienced! We enjoyed this blessing of another Godwink and sign from heaven.

2/9/2020
6:43 a.m.

I just woke up from a dream after having another dream, but this one I'll remember because I'm documenting it. My dream has significance and I believe contains an important message—a message from God, our Heavenly Father. I dreamt that I went to an event to hear a speaker. Terry was meeting me there, which he did. The house unfolded into a large room that appeared to be in the setting of a huge meeting room that reminded me of a church. The crowd was initially smaller, but it grew and grew as more people gathered. After the presentation, Terry left to return to work. My cousins, who I ran into, offered to give me a ride. While driving back, we hit a snow drift, and the car landed off the road. We were right by a shop, so we decided to check it out. We had to go under a bridge and through a tunnel to get there. We learned someone had purchased a portion of the land under the bridge because it had its own little store with items to purchase. We guessed not the owner but someone else discovered these and decided to call them their own. As we walked past these items and under the road to the other side, there was a home and shop where guests could stay. They had loads of gifts made out of different candies and, while really cute, they were also pricey. It appeared that the woman who ran the shop was ill or had passed, so her family was selling out the items. I left quickly to meet up with the others, only to realize they'd left! I believe I was offered another ride with four women who were heading to town. I asked if they would please take me back to the venue where we'd heard the speaker. When they agreed, we backtracked and finally got there. I was left feeling overwhelmed without my car, purse, or phone, but I realized while it appeared I'd lost everything, I would always have my faith and my story. This I could share with anyone, offering them hope. What a beautiful way to feel fulfilled as a disciple of God and serve in the capacity I desired and He desired. God is good. He gave me reassurance in my dream what while it appeared I'd lost everything, with Him and only Him I have everything! My heart is full! It's a Godwink for certain. I trust this completely!

4/5/2020

Started in meditation and prayer today, then rested in God's love and listened. God said that I need to forgive the guilt I'm holding on to. Ben's death was a suicide, and I'm acting as if it was a homicide and I am the guilty party. I'm not. I reached out throughout the day of November 11, 2014. Ben knew I was here, and he knew my love for him. I need to release this burden to free myself and move forward and live with joy in my life. This is what God desires: not fleeting moments of happiness, but actual sustained joy that comes from knowing God. This is what God wants for me and for our entire family.

9/3/2020

Received some signs today on our anniversary. First, I noticed Ben's bank statement generated, which was a hello from Ben. Then while *reading the Family Life daily devotion, it referenced "everyone in need of hope." Rings a bell for BENS Hope. Heard the song "Blessings" on the radio, loved the timing. Saw a feather in the driveway as I was coming into the garage. After Pam and Bruce left tonight, it was 11:11 p.m., the same number as Ben's Angelversary. Getting ready to leave for Chetek, I came across an anniversary card from our kids for our twenty-nineth anniversary that included a message and signature from each of our kids. Then I found an email from 2012 with correspondence from Ben, specific to visiting him on our way back from Chetek. Pretty powerful sign since we were just heading off to Chetek today! Terry found a dime walking into a store! Mom had a tomato in the shape of a heart. How's that for signs?!*

November 2020

Mandy, Carrie, Terry, and I agreed to doing virtual presentations in Mount Horeb this year since COVID-19 prevented us from doing in-person visits. Since neither of us are tech-savvy and the girls were joining us from their locations in Madison, we were nervous about glitches on our end. That was apparent to Terry's boss on the grounds crew, so much so that he asked Terry that morning while they were picking up trash what was going on. Terry explained his anxiety about us partaking in virtual presentations, and as he did, his boss picked up a piece of paper from the ground. It was handwritten in marker. After opening and reading it, he handed the paper to Terry. The note read: Be anxious for nothing, but in everything by prayer and supplication, with thanksgiving, let your requests be made known to God; and the peace of God, which surpasses all understanding, will guard your hearts and your minds through Christ Jesus. Philippians 4:6-7 (NKJV)

Terry brought this home and handed it to me when I walked in the door. I was feeling anxious myself as we were getting ready to go live with the virtual presentations. Of course, I wept then thanked God for this Godwink at the exact moment we needed it. That's how great our God is!

11/11/20

On Ben's six-year Angelversary, I spent the day with Pam. I woke up after having a visit/dream experience with Benjamin. I miss him terribly. There were lots of tears before Pam and I even started our day. We stopped and picked up flowers to take to the cemetery, where more tears were shed. This is my new reality. After leaving the cemetery, Pam and I headed onward to Dubuque. We stopped at J & J Consignment and spent a couple hours walking around. Even though I'd made laps several times, I felt guided to make one more. As I did, I came across a plaque that caught my eye. The plaque had a poem on it called "Ascension" by Colleen Hitchcock and was dated 1987, the year Ben was born. The poem on it read:

Ascension

And if I go,

while you're still here . . .

Know that I live on,

vibrating to a different measure,

—behind a thin veil you cannot see through.

You will not see me,

so you must have faith.

I wait for the time when we can soar together again,

—both aware of each other.

Until then, live your life to its fullest.

And when you need me,

Just whisper my name in your heart,

. . . I will be there.

I wondered how I missed this earlier and was grateful I was guided back to it. As I read this poem, tears streamed down my face. I felt like Ben was talking to me. I felt such a yearning for Ben and such sadness, but at the same time, this poem also offered such comfort.

As Pam and I drove back into Platteville after our day in Dubuque, we were reminiscing about the blessing of this plaque. At that moment, "Come as You Are" came on the radio. We both looked at each other with open mouths. It is our signature song for BENS Hope events and a song initially heard by our brother-in-law, Ken. Interestingly enough, God put it on Ken's heart to learn this song. He accomplished that, and coincidentally, that was the song we chose to play at Ben's funeral. Ken was gracious and agreed to sing it. Ken knew there was a reason God directed him to learn this song ahead of Ben's death. Does it make you wonder? I hope so. For me, I believe God delivers these Godwinks to validate His love and presence in our lives.

Later, I reached out to Colleen Hitchcock to inquire about getting additional prints of her poem, sharing how I'd discovered it and the significance of its meaning on Ben's Angelversary. Imagine my delight when Colleen shared in return that she dates her work, and this one was dated 11/11. Coincidence? I think not.

11/29/2020

Another Godwink happened this Sunday. I had another dream about Ben. He was really busy, working in a lofted area in a big space. Ben doesn't typically make eye contact with me in my dreams, but he has on a few occasions. This was not one of them. What I did notice were many treasures like gems, stones, and things of value being uncovered throughout heaven. I never determined if they were Ben's treasures, my treasures, or treasures hidden in heaven.

Terry and I headed to the store later that morning to pick up additional lights since we were outside decorating for Christmas. As we were standing in the checkout, I noticed a DVD on top that read, "For the Love of Ben." It was a DVD of Benji the pup, but the sticker covered the "ji" part, just leaving Ben. I started to text the girls to share about the dream I'd had and now this DVD. I was texting as Terry finished checking out, then we walked outside to our vehicle. I had to wait until I got into the vehicle to finish the message. After I finally sent it, Mandy responded, informing me of another sign. I'd sent this text at 11:11...Ben's Angelversary! Another

Godwink!

When we got home, Terry and I resumed decorating outside as we listened to the Family Life Radio station blaring from the stereo in our garage. Our neighbor walked over to visit, and as I shared these Godwinks, as if on cue, "Come as You Are" came on the radio. I mean seriously, you cannot make these things up!

10/31/2021

Found a bookmark tonight made with roses from Ben's funeral. Felt it was a hello from Ben to acknowledge the early arrival of grandbaby Desi, All Saints' Day, or Halloween, but not for sure. Did give thanks for receiving this sign.

11/4/2021

After presenting to two classes in Mount Horeb High School, we stopped at Sunn Cafe for lunch before coming home at 1:00 p.m. Terry had the afternoon off, and I intended to go back to work. I lost it a couple of times during our presentations and found I just needed to take a few moments to focus on breathing. But after just sharing with the students the importance of listening to "the voice within," I took my own advice, remembering that God will give me rest. I stayed in the dress I'd worn today, and I crawled into bed. I fell asleep within moments and slept until 3:45 p.m. I was shocked when I woke up, realizing how long I'd slept, but obviously it was needed. I felt rested, peaceful, and loved upon waking up. I decided to take an Epsom salt bath next.

Took the book Why Me to read while I soaked in the tub. I was reflecting on presentations, thinking of Ben, and thanking God for giving me/us the strength for this emotional day. In addition, our grandbaby, Desi, decided to make her appearance recently and arrived six weeks early, and with that came worries and concerns for Carrie. Ben's Angelversary was also on the horizon. As I was reflecting and offering prayers of gratitude during my bath, I witnessed two heart-shaped bubble formations, one smaller and the second one larger. I watched as these two bubbles moved toward each other, the only two bubbles in my view. As I offered a prayer of thanksgiving, these two bubbles merged, and I wept! Once again, I was reminded that Ben is with me, and God is too! They're always holding me up. Later at bedtime, I awoke from a dream, or so I thought, to a light show! At first, I thought car lights were coming through the blinds that were open, but the blinds were closed. Then I wondered if my retina was detaching! These lights spiraled around whimsically, and I sat up to ensure I was not dreaming. I was awake! I felt the most beautiful sense of being held and loved, and I felt peaceful. I thanked God again for His presence and tremendous love.

November 2021

I've always wanted to recreate the journey of going to Ben's place in La Crosse. I told myself, you can go, but he's not going to be there. So for me, a huge experience of working through the grieving process was returning to La Crosse. I saw so many Godwinks when we were there. My favorite Godwink was when Mandy, Carrie, Mom, and I were trying to decide on where to eat the last night we were in town. We ended up venturing to Piggy's, a well-known restaurant near the Mississippi River in downtown La Crosse. Going to Piggy's was a first for all of us, and we booked a late reservation. Imagine our surprise as we pulled up and saw the Kaplan building next to it. Kaplan is where Ben worked. After our incredible dining experience, which we felt like Ben had joined us for, we went outside. While inside Piggy's, we saw a sign from the table we were seated at, and I wanted to get it on video. Mandy ended up taking the video for me. Somehow she didn't notice while taking the video that an orb was dashing around, and she captured it in the video. Aw, hello, Ben!

This venture with my mom and my girls was something difficult yet so meaningful. The purpose of this trip was for me to make new, happy memories and not be in this place of such desperation and sadness. I couldn't even think about La Crosse before this without it tearing my heart out. I felt very guided by God. He was saying, "You need to do this," because when I try to push away those thoughts and past experiences, they just resurface over and over and over. When I had the courage to go forward, it was surprising how I didn't have the weight on my heart or the fear in my mind because I elected to address those feelings. Does making these new memories mean I no longer think about Ben when I go to La Crosse? Absolutely not! But taking the route that Mom and I did, driving directly to his old apartment, allowed me to cry my way through those feelings. Knowing his car wasn't in the garage and that Ben wasn't going to be running down the steps to greet me was agonizing. I did take photographs to capture this memory of that experience. For me, it was such a big feat to accomplish. And I know it was something that really helped lighten my heart.

The following are Godwinks that Carrie and Mandy received that they described as divinely orchestrated.

CARRIE

I kept seeing the time 9:11 in the weeks leading up to Ben dying.

"My mind is free" and, "It's not your fault," were written on two angel cards Mom got the night Ben died.

We went to Erschen's for flowers. The store was decorated in red and green and white and blue for Christmas. I walked over to where we were supposed to be looking at flowers and right there was an old chair all wrapped in purple, sparkly tulle with a purple bow on it.

Two nights after Ben died, Matt and I were in my bed watching SATC, and I noticed for the first time that I had a dead pixel in my TV.

11/14/2014
Mandy and I went to her apartment for the first time since Ben died, and her heat wouldn't work, her computer had developed a virus, and her smoke alarm wouldn't stop beeping.

I texted Mom a comforting message about Ben being happy now, and after I sent it, Pam replied by saying it was her and asking if I wanted her to share it with Mom. That was confusing. The time was 9:11.

Mandy went to pick up a book on hold at the library. She had received an email from the library saying to come pick it up, but it wasn't there. It was missing. The book was called May Cause Miracles.

A few days after Ben's death, Mandy went to Walgreens to get a prescription. The pharmacy computer showed Mandy had two insurance policies, and she couldn't get her prescription. Mandy had to call her insurance. I laughed as she was on the phone. It was another "technical difficulty."

A lady delivered flowers from the Smith family to our house in the evening. She wore a purple coat that had an angel pin. She told us she had also lost a son to suicide. As she kept talking, we discovered she was Mary Kay's second cousin. (Mary Kay and her husband Kim are good friends of our family.) Their grandpas were brothers. Mary Kay hadn't seen her since she was a kid. This woman had wise words for Mom, telling her depression is just like a disease, much like heart disease. She also said that a doctor could have been standing at Ben's side and still wouldn't have been able to do anything to help him. People with depression are victims. It's not their choice. Sadly, they can die from this disease.

11/13/2014

She came back to talk to us after she closed the flower shop. Her son had been missing for a week before they knew he died. She and Grandma both lost sons in eighth grade. Another son who she lost had the death date of Abby's birthday, December 6.

Mary Kay and Kim tried to check in to Country Inn & Suites. The computers were down, and it would have taken at least forty-five minutes before they could get checked in. They went to a different hotel. That hotel just had a cancellation and were able to give them a room.

I looked at a family photo of our family and noticed something I hadn't really realized before. We were all supposed to be looking at each other while laughing. Ben was the only one looking forward, and we were all smiling and looking at Ben.

MANDY

11/24/2014

I was playing Words with Friends against the computer. First, I noticed that my letters spelled out "sorrywi." I also noticed it made the word "worry." It was interesting and reminded me of Ben (because everything does). Then I played a word, and the computer played the word "Ben." That was a proper noun and wasn't allowed in the game, but there it was. Apparently, I was playing against Ben (it was the computer version, so I wasn't surprised). I got new letters, and the next word I saw was "glory." Interesting. This all came after I dreamed about Ben last night.

12/1/2014

I continued to play Words with Friends against the computer—which referred itself as <u>Solo</u> Play—which reminded me of Ben's computer name, Oneself. I then witnessed the computer play these words: "Ben," "Beano," "via"—which reminded me of the audio from his twenty-first birthday and made me laugh out loud—and "amen." These words came throughout the course of a few weeks. Also, last night I dreamed about Ben the entire night. The dreams have switched from scary to sad. It must be my way of addressing my feelings and moving through the grieving process. I've been seeing 11/11 a lot lately, whether it's the time or a price or whatever...it's the date Ben died. I don't like being reminded of it. I will look up number meanings when I go home.

1/9/2015

Two nights ago, I met my new nanny family and watched little Sebastian (also the name of our old dog, whom Ben loved). I was talking with Corey and Ryan (the parents) about the holidays and told them I'd recently lost my brother. They explained their aunt and uncle were having a tough time too, as they had lost their son recently. His name was Ben. And he was 27. Same name and age as my brother. It caught me off guard, and I got a little emotional. Mom says it's a sign. Pretty literal sign. I'm still dreaming about Ben weekly. (Side note—two nights ago, I dreamed about Grandpa holding a little baby.) Last night's dream was about (healthy) Ben having this beautiful, clear, heart-shaped, smooth stone-looking thing. He was protecting it in a black, velvet case I think, and I think he was trying to give it to someone he loved or saving it for someone he loved. I don't know if it was intended for his wife or for Mom or who. This showed his gentle side, which reminded me how much I do miss him. He was so kind and caring and sweet. I almost feel like I no longer have time to be sad about him because if I really, really thought about how much he was a part of my life and is now just GONE, I would fall apart. It's such a disappointing realization. Heartbreaking. Maybe I'm coming out of my numbness. There are no more holidays for distraction.

4/27/2015

I am working at Midwest Title now and taking on new challenges. One of the files had a lender from Onalaska with a closing date of March 5 (Ben's birthday). Hey, Ben. I've had lots of dreams and reminders of him the past few weeks, everywhere and pretty regularly. It's comforting, as there'd been a span when I wasn't dreaming of him too often. He's back in an obvious way, I just miss his physical presence so much...

5/7/2015

Life is sort of falling into place for me. Maybe this loss has helped me focus on what's really important in life and not worry about pleasing others. LOTS of 333s lately, but mostly just yesterday and today. Makes me wonder if something's going to happen or if I'm just being reminded that Ben and Grandpa are around.

5/12/15

Last night I finally realized why I was seeing 627 ALL the time since

Ben's death. That is sort of my number for him (like 333 was for Grandpa). Well anyway, obviously it's my birth date, but I wondered what it had to do with me. Then as I was doing a Jillian workout video in my living room last night (exactly six months after Ben's death), I saw 627 on my stove, and it all made sense; Ben wants me to focus on ME: on self-improvement, on self-love, and on all that goes with it. I've been on this difficult path but am really becoming a great version of myself. Granted, there are things I need to work on, but I feel like the genuine Mandy I really am.

It was a definite AHA! moment for me. Very cool. And of course, it was so selfless of Ben to be constantly reminding me that his loss will ultimately help me find myself. Powerful stuff.

1/19/2016

And now after all this time, I've become a person whom I admire. I love myself and am happy with where I'm at in life. I am with a man I love and am pursuing a career I'm passionate about. Would I have gotten here without losing Ben? Maybe not as quickly. I almost feel guilty for this growth. I am overall a better person, living every day to become the best version of myself and continuing to be my authentic self. I still miss Ben, and every single day, something reminds me of him. I am sometimes sad, sometimes mad, other times happy, and maybe, at times, empty. I realized this morning that losing Ben won't be my only tragedy to deal with in this life. I will undoubtedly lose other family members, friends, and loved ones. I'll also encounter stress, dilemmas, and dramas that are beyond my current comprehension. Knowing that fact somehow prepares me for the road ahead. Life is a tough ride, tougher than I thought. But I am tough too. Tougher than I thought.

1/25/2016

I dreamed about Ben last night. We were having a regular conversation, just talking about new cell phones, and his had some new technology on it that I didn't know about (go figure). It was nice to see him. I enjoyed the feeling I had of us hanging out. It was just like he was here.

CHAPTER 14

JUST A THOUGHT AND PATTI-ISMS

I realize the contents of this book may weigh heavy on your heart. I mean, the book is about suicide, right? Anyway, I wanted to close on a note that God put on my heart in the middle of the night. They are what I consider "just a thought" or as Rebecca, my editor, referred to as "Patti-isms." I hope as you read them that you take time to reflect on the significance they may have in your life. I pray they offer truth, bring joy, and encourage kindness.

> *How are you today? Good? Fine? OK? These are responses we may hear in passing. However, if you answer honestly, I might hear "tired," "sad," "lonely," "overwhelmed," "stressed," "depleted," or "worried." Please know it's OK to not be OK.*

> *I love exchanging hugs! Did you realize it's an act of giving where you receive as well? Offer a hug today!*

> *Be an example. Spread kindness.*

> *Each of us has our own "sole" journey—it really is a "soul" journey.*

> *Life isn't always fair, but it still offers blessings.*

I wish the world would treat others the way they hope people will treat their children/grandchildren/pets.

Forgiveness lightens YOUR heart.

A smile goes a long way.

I pretend the slow senior driving in front of me is one of my grandparents.

Another person's perception is not your reality; it's their reality.

People only know what they know.

People only understand what they've experienced.

Father, forgive them, they know not what they do.

What goodness comes from holding a grudge?

I wish people put as much energy into loving as hating; love thy neighbor.

Even if you don't understand mental health, please have compassion for those struggling with it.

Don't wish you'd had more time with someone, make the time to be with them now.

If someone calls in sick from work, ask them if they're OK.

Help can arrive when you are honest with how you're truly feeling.

*It's alright to be vulnerable. il others are uncomfortable with it, that's **their** problem.*

*Hurt people **hurt** people.*

You are beautiful and wonderful, and if you weren't here, someone would miss you with all their heart.

Suicide is not contagious.

People don't wish to die, they only want their pain to end.

If you want to heal, you'll have to deal and feel.

*You're not responsible for another person's actions. However, you **are** responsible for how you respond.*

Never say never.

Each grieving process is as unique as each person and their circumstances.

Sometimes the only way to see the light is by walking through the darkness.

Thy will be done, not my will.

You don't have to deal with your grief now; It'll wait for you.
—Terry Cullen

God didn't put you here to be a spectator. He wants you in the game! —Rebecca Spindler, editor

In sharing my story, my wish for this book is to help bring peace to anyone who is a survivor of suicide. I also pray that this book brings hope and support to anyone who is struggling. I pray it offers insight whether you've experienced a suicide loss or not. I hope that suicide can become a topic of conversation versus one that is avoided at all costs. I pray for those in deep despair to remember you are not alone. If *Tears of Love* can offer insight on the aftermath of suicide to someone contemplating suicide or to someone who has experienced the loss of their loved one by suicide, then my expectation for this book has succeeded.

People desire to find purpose in life and leave a legacy. I feel my circumstances led me to my purpose that God chose me for. I am grateful God put it on my heart to write *Tears of Love*: a legacy for those in this world. It will be humbling and honoring to know that this book exists in my lifetime on this earth and when I'm in heaven with our Heavenly Father and reunited with my loved ones. I pray you come across it at the right moment; call it a Godwink if you will. In reading it, may you find insight, answers, and the hope you seek. God Bless you. —Patti

To learn more about the BENS Hope organization, request a speaking engagement, schedule an in-person or Zoom meeting, attend an upcoming retreat or other offered event, or make a donation, please visit www.bens-hope.org.

THANK YOU

I would like to express my sincere gratitude toward individuals who have been instrumental on my journey, offering continued support, especially since Ben's suicide November 11, 2014. I also extend my deepest appreciation for those offering support while I was writing this book and all their patience, love, and understanding it took in doing this. I am still in awe that *Tears of Love* came to fruition, but then again, why should I be? I mean, God instructed me to write *Tears of Love*, saying it will save the lives of others. And I know thy will be done, not my will. I trust God because He has been the one and only constant in my life. If you want someone dependable, reliable, and available 24/7, I encourage you to come to know our Heavenly Father, who not only offers His support during our lifetime on this earth, but for those of us who believe, grants us eternal bliss in heaven with Him. When God asked me to write this book, stating that it will save lives— as I've referenced countless times throughout—it wasn't until I was working on this thank you section, specifically while I was reading the Bible this morning, that God put it on my heart that this book will save lives because of those who come to know Him. As much as I've shared my story and the significance He has had in my life, He wishes to take part in yours, too. Regardless of your past, His miracles of forgiveness bring healing, wholeness, and changed lives to those who trust Him.

Ask and it will be given to you; seek and you will find; knock and the door will be opened to you. For everyone who asks receives; the one who seeks finds; and to the one who knocks, the door will be opened.
Matthew 7:7-8 (NIV)

First and foremost, thank you, God, for your command in writing this book and putting people in my life to see *Tears of Love* come to fruition. You are my Lord and Savior.

Thank you, my wonderful family—in heaven and on earth—and my friends for your love, support, and encouragement over the years and especially since Ben's death. It means so very much!

Thank you to those who have and continue to support our efforts through BENS Hope.

Thank you to Ben's friends and family who contributed to *Tears of Love*.

Thank you, courageous attendees at SOS who share your hearts, stories, laughter, and tears.

Thank you, Pastor Mark and our church families at Bethlehem E&R Church and Lancaster Congregational Church.

Thank you, all who have prayed for us and our efforts through BENS Hope.

Thank you, Sister Kay and Sister Marie and all our treasured friends at the Sisters of the Presentation.

Thank you to my wonderful, patient, insightful, caring, faith-filled publisher, Kristin from Little Creek Press and Book Design, who believed my story was book-worthy.

Thank you to my editor, Rebecca Williams Spindler from Spindler Writing, for all your support, love, and contributions, and especially your gift and vision in taking my journal entries and creating *Tears of Love*. You made this happen!

Thank you, Heidi Overson, a writer, editor, and my proofreader whom God brought into my life for more purposes than proofreading *Tears of Love*. Sharing our hurts, hearts, and truths has been a tremendous blessing.

There are not enough words to express my sincere appreciation and gratitude for the support and constant cheerleading, guidance, direction, conversations, insight, suggestions, and support that you've provided. Thank you from the bottom of my heart, Tammy Salmon-Stephens, my life coach who has been instrumental in guiding our family, helping us with outreach efforts through BENS Hope, and who has been my cheerleader, meeting with me bimonthly these past years, encouraging me, believing in me, and ensuring *Tears of Love* came to fruition. You are a blessing beyond words.

And thank you, Benjamin, for the blessing of being my firstborn and only son. You were a light in my life when you were here and still are in your absence. I am honored God chose me to be your mom. I love you so much and miss you every day. In your suicide note, you apologized, saying, "It was not you who failed me, Mom, but I that failed you." Benjamin, you could never fail me, honey. You were selfless, kind, loyal, loving, free of judgment, and giving, always giving without ever expecting anything in return. You not only gave in your lifetime but also in your death—you are still giving.

Dear Ben,

I pray, Benjamin, that you are proud of the work we are doing through BENS Hope in your honor. Words cannot express the depth of pain we've experienced losing you, but through our faith, we are moving forward to find goodness by helping others struggling. We love you and miss you. We trust in God's plan and the work we are doing here. We know that one day God will reunite us with you in heaven. What a day it will be to see you again, my son. I love you more always.

Mom

ABOUT THE AUTHOR

Patti Cullen, a Wisconsin native, married her high school sweetheart, Terry, in 1983. They had three children, Ben, Mandy, and Carrie, their greatest blessings! Life was good! However, on November 11, 2014, life as they knew it changed in an instant. On this date, they learned their son took his life by suicide. This was the reason that BENS Hope came to fruition.

After a 43-year banking career, giving approximately 300 suicide-awareness-prevention presentations, and authoring the book *Tears of Love*, Patti resigned from her banking career to serve in the capacity God put on her heart as a Grief, Grace and Gratitude Specialist.

Patti and Terry continue their mission of educating others to aid in suicide awareness-prevention, reduce the stigma of suicide, offer support through their monthly Survivors of Suicide meetings, and provide resources and tools for those struggling.

Why, you may ask? Because Everyone Needs Some Hope!

Printed in the USA
CPSIA information can be obtained
at www.ICGtesting.com
JSHW021059121123
51902JS00004B/27

9 781955 656665